The Successful Christian Life

Elmer L. Towns

ACCENT BOOKS
A division of Accent-B/P Publications, Inc.
12100 W. Sixth Avenue
P.O. Box 15337
Denver, Colorado 80215

Printed in the United States of America

Library of Congress Catalog Card Number: 79-52538

ISBN 0-89636-027-X

CONTENTS

PREFACE
A Fresh Start in Life 5

PART I
COMING TO KNOW THE SAVIOUR 11

Chapter 1
What You Did to Become a Christian 13

Chapter 2
What God Did to Save You 23

PART II
GETTING STARTED RIGHT
IN THE CHRISTIAN LIFE 35

Chapter 3
Be Sure of Your Salvation 37

Chapter 4
Become Grounded on the Word of God 53

Chapter 5
Make Prayer a Regular Part of Your Life 69

PART III
FELLOWSHIPPING WITH A CHURCH 85

Chapter 6
Your First Public Act Is Baptism 87

Chapter 7
Why You Should Be Related to a Church 97

Chapter 8
Your Ultimate Step of Obedience 109

PART IV
SERVING THE LORD SUCCESSFULLY 119

Chapter 9
Victory Over Sin Is Promised You 121

Chapter 10
Knowing God's Will for Your Life 137

Chapter 11
Getting God's Power for Service 151

Chapter 12
Winning Others to Christ 165

PART V
DEVELOPING INNER VIRTUES 173

Chapter 13
Be Motivated by Faith, Love, Hope 175

Chapter 14
Be Faithful All Your Days 187

Preface

A Fresh Start in Life

The True Story of One Woman Who Found Christ

When I was twelve I really wanted to do whatever you were supposed to do to get right with God. I didn't love God, but I had a deep respect for Him.

At that time my family was going to a church where the main emphasis seemed to be that you had to be baptized for remission of sins. I thought that if I was baptized everything would be OK—that would make me a Christian and that's what "good" people were—but I was afraid to get up in front of all those people; I didn't want to get wet and ugly.

We were told that Jesus died for our sins, but I really didn't think I was a sinner because I'd always tried to be a good person. The important thing seemed to be getting baptized.

I knew the procedure from watching from the pew on Sunday mornings. The minister would ask for people to come forward. I knew once you were up there, he'd ask you if you believed Jesus was the Son of God. You would say yes and get baptized. It all went very quickly; the congregation waited while you put on a robe. Then you were brought into the baptistry and submerged before them.

Finally I went forward, said yes, and was baptized. I also found out afterwards that in being baptized I had become a member of the church, but I really didn't care about that at the time. I was just relieved to have the whole experience over. Now I felt like an official Christian.

My major experience with Bibles had been memorizing verses for gold stars when I was younger. I did have a pretty white Bible with my name on it that I enjoyed carrying around at church. But I didn't read it because I couldn't understand it.

We didn't spend any more time at church than we had to. We'd go for a morning service on Sunday, then leave as quickly as we could get through all of the handshaking and smiling. The people looked friendly, but I didn't like being there. The outside church door meant freedom.

Years passed and I was in college. I studied hard and was still a good Christian person in my own mind. However, by this time I wasn't so sure about God, and Jesus had become a name in history. Just in case, I kept praying and ended the prayer by saying, "in Jesus' name." I never understood why; it was just a formula.

While in college, my friends and I became interested in palm reading, astrology, astro-projection, and ESP. We "played" with a Ouija board and knew someone who used Tarot cards. Two of us signed up to check out the Rosicrucians. We were researching reincarnation and finding out about the Bahai faith.

I still considered myself a Christian, and had no idea that these activities could be of Satan. I didn't even believe there was a real devil. After all, he was a red guy with horns and a tail, like kids dressed up on Halloween.

I graduated from a state university, then taught first grade for several years and a learning disability class for one year. I liked the children, teachers, parents and everyone, but I was really restless.

By now, I knew by observation and experience that job security, money, possessions and friends were not enough to make me happy. Although I was single, I knew enough married friends to see that marriage wasn't a guarantee of happiness, either. So what was the point of it all? Why were we here anyway?

People thought I was a happy person, but the only time I was really happy was when I was alone in the mountains with the quiet and the trees. Even there, though, the questions kept coming.

I quit teaching and went back to college, majoring in art. I asked a lot more questions but no one seemed to have any satisfactory answers. There were a lot of people "doing their own thing" but I saw that just doing what you thought you wanted to do didn't really make you happy either.

While I was still enrolled as an art student, my friend Nancy became very depressed. We talked a lot but I couldn't think of any way to help her. Meanwhile, another friend told Nancy about a Bible-believing church. The pastor could help, she said. Going to see him seemed like a good idea; we sure didn't have any other solutions. I thought, if God is real maybe He will help.

Nancy talked with the pastor, started going to church and, unknown to me, accepted Jesus as her Saviour. Then she invited me to visit the church.

Because Nancy was feeling better and the people seemed to be friendly, to care about other people, I thought I'd try it. I don't remember what the pastor said that day but I knew he believed what he was preaching. It wasn't a dry lecture; he was actually teaching from the Bible. And the Bible didn't seem to be a lot of dry words; it was exciting and the words were answering my questions. I was hungry for more. I hated to leave that Sunday morning and waited in anticipation for that night. Then we discovered we could come on Wednesday, too. Even with Sunday School class, then church in the morning and evening, I couldn't seem to get enough.

A few evenings later I was alone at home reading, checking the pastor's quotations against the Bible I had; I didn't want to be tricked. For the first time I understood *how* a person actually became a Christian! I didn't understand why the Bible said the things it did; I just knew it said them. That night I really believed the Bible was from God.

I only knew God as the Father so I talked with Him, reading I John 3:23 and I John 5:11-13. I read more of what the Bible said; there was Jesus all over the place. He was *really* God's Son. I didn't know all of that was in the Bible.

I sat at the dining room table and said OK to God. The pastor had said all you had to do to have Jesus come into your life was to ask Him; you didn't have to feel anything, just know that He'd come because He said He would. You had to admit you were a sinner and ask Him to forgive you—and He would.

I didn't *feel* like a sinner, but the Bible said by God's standards I was, so I asked Him to forgive me. To the best of my understanding, I asked Jesus into my life. I was afraid, but I asked God to be in charge of everything. I explained to Him that He would have to prove everything to me because I knew so little and this was all so new.

The pastor said you didn't *have* to feel anything, but I did. I felt relieved and I felt protected. I felt like I belonged to God and I felt safe from Satan. God had led me right up to the entrance into His family, showed me how to get in, then helped me trust Him so He could come into my life and bring me into His Life. He had always been there to help me; I just hadn't known it!

At first the church and the pastor and the fellowship were my lifeline. Gradually, I learned to have the Lord teach me directly through His Word, along with life experiences. But my church is still my favorite place on this earth except for the times I'm alone with the Bible and the Lord.

When I first asked Jesus into my life and understood that He actually loved *me,* I hoped He would come right away so somehow I could be with Him. Really, the only reason I could see for staying on earth was that some other people needed to know about Him. I was ready to go.

Now since I've known the Lord, He has been doing real changing in me. I can see why I needed to be doing some growing and learning. He has changed and is still changing me. I am becoming a new person. This is the most exciting adventure of all! It is not easy because I try too hard and get in the way. I also seem to be fairly stubborn in some areas.

I've really had some great teaching at the church and I feel the understanding growing. The whole process is fantastic and it's Him. One of the best things that has happened is that I am now learning to relax a little in Christ and maybe let Him do whatever needs doing a little faster. As I said, I'm a real "do it yourself" type, only that's not how He works.

How can I say thanks for a new life? Where do I begin? I praise the Lord for His people and His pastors. I'm glad I had a fresh start in life! All I can say is PRAISE THE LORD.

PART I

Coming to Know the Saviour

Chapter 1
What You Did To Become a Christian

During the Second World War, Joel Ortendahl knelt in the bottom of a foxhole. When the Germans advanced, he was scared. Remembering verses from the Bible his grandmother had read to him, he received Christ as his Saviour and now testifies that he was saved at that moment. It took several years before he began to walk with God, but ultimately he became a preacher.

James Mastin sat in New Testament Baptist Church, Miami, with a number of other junior boys. The Sunday School teacher asked him if he wanted to go forward. Embarrassed, he did—not because he had volunteered but because he had been taught to respond to adults. Even though it was at the prodding of an adult, young James sincerely received the Lord; he too became a minister and now pastors Central Baptist Church, Milwaukee, Wisconsin.

Florence Smith described herself as being on the bottom rung of the ladder of society. She drank incessantly in her trailer in the backwoods of Virginia. She contemplated suicide and went so far as to take a pistol to a small gravel pit where she planned to commit the deed. There she decided to give God a chance. For two or three weeks she listened to every radio preacher she could find and did everything they all commanded. She repeated the "sinner's prayer" but knew in her heart she was not saved.

Finally she went to a nearby church that preached the gospel. During the invitation she started forward and later testified, "God saved me as I turned from the pew to walk down the aisle." Even though she again repeated the sinner's prayer at the altar, she testified God saved her at the moment she responded and began walking forward. It was an act of faith that did it.

Ruth Jeane Forbes received the Lord when she came home from Sunday School where they had talked about having a "dirty" heart. She wanted Jesus to clean her heart, and as a five-year-old, she knelt by her mother's knee and received Christ as her Saviour. She grew up to live for Christ.

Every one of these stories is different. Each person's experience is different, and the story of how you were saved may be different from any of these. Yet God does not save people differently. Some were saved after a person talked with them. Others were saved when they were alone. Some listened to a sermon; others had not heard a sermon in years. Some were embarrassed; others were afraid. Florence Smith prayed the right words, but it didn't work for her at that time. Why? What are the ingredients of salvation?

THE WAY OF SALVATION

Salvation is as simple as a relationship with Jesus Christ; you put your faith in Him. The Bible says, "Look . . . and be . . . saved" (Isaiah 45:22). Look and live. When you look to Him to answer your sin problem, you live for eternity. Yet the theologians have made salvation complicated.

Not every church member will go to Heaven; yet most have declared they believe in God. "Many will say to me in that day, Lord, Lord, have we not . . . in thy name done many wonderful works? And then will I profess unto them, I never knew you: depart from me, ye that work iniquity" (Matthew 7:22-23). Obviously, some people who think they are going to Heaven will not make it. They know the "religious" answers, but that is not enough.

Salvation is pictured as a road; you take steps along this road to get to Heaven. Jesus said, "Enter ye in at the strait gate: for wide is the gate, and broad is the way, that leadeth to destruction, and many there be which go in thereat: Because strait is the gate, and narrow is the way, which leadeth unto life, and few there be that find it" (Matthew 7:13-14).

In the book of Acts, early Christianity was referred to as the "way" (9:2). It is the "way" to God. In approaching God you must take four steps; you need no more and can take no less.

1. *Know your need.* People do not turn to God until they feel a need for Him. And this compulsion is not felt until they realize that their paths will lead to destruction. God says, "For all have sinned, and come short of the glory of God" (Romans 3:23). The word "all" includes every human of all ages.

A minister once tried to convince a small boy he was a sinner, but the boy would not admit it.

"Have you ever lied to Mommy?" the preacher asked. The boy shook his head no.

"Have you ever taken anything that didn't belong to you or fought with your brother or sister?" Again the boy shook his head no.

"He's sinning to you now," observed his older brother.

He knew his little brother was guilty of these actions. The Bible says we ALL have sinned. A man will never turn to God until he first realizes he is a sinner.

2. *Know your punishment.* In our society we usually don't worry about people who break the law until they hurt someone else, but God's laws are different. He said, "For the wages of sin is death; but the gift of God is eternal life through Jesus Christ our Lord" (Romans 6:23). God punishes every offense. Because you have sinned, you must pay the penalty.

When you break a speed law, you don't get caught for every offense, but if you speed through a radar trap, unless you are a good talker, you pay the fine. Along this line of thought, you never escape God's radar for He catches every offense; and the penalty is death.

"Even for one sin?" a woman asked at the church altar. The soul-winner showed her, "For whosoever shall keep the whole law, and yet offend in one point, he is guilty of all" (James 2:10). *One* sin makes you a sinner.

"The wages of sin is death" (Romans 6:23a). You get wages for your work; *wages* are what you have coming to you. This verse shows that you have death or hell coming because you have sinned. In contrast, ". . . the gift of God is eternal life . . ." (6:23b). The gift is free and undeserved; it is not wages. You get death for your sins, yet God gives you life as a *gift*.

3. *Know the gospel.* "But God commendeth his love toward us, in that, while we were yet sinners, Christ died

for us" (Romans 5:8). The word *commendeth* means "to give." God has given His Son to die for our sins. This is the gospel. *Gospel* means "good news," and the greatest news ever is that God saves man.

The gospel has two aspects: propositional truth and personal truth. First, propositional truth reflects the truth on paper—it is written in our doctrinal statements. This is the gospel which is God's plan for salvation. Paul defined it: "I declare unto you the gospel which I preached unto you, which also ye have received, and wherein ye stand; By which also ye are saved . . . that Christ died for our sins according to the scriptures; And that he was buried, and that he rose again the third day according to the scriptures" (I Corinthians 15:1-4). The gospel explains the death, burial, and resurrection of Jesus Christ. He died for us.

4. *Respond to the gospel.* The gospel is more than propositional truth; it is personal truth. This means truth exists in a person, the person Jesus Christ. When you accept this truth, you do more than give mental assent to His death, burial, and resurrection. You accept Christ as your Saviour. The gospel becomes personal when you invite Christ into your life. "But as many as received him [Christ], to them gave he power to become the sons of God" (John 1:12).

Some have a correct doctrinal statement, but if they do not have the person Jesus Christ in their hearts, they are wrong—dead wrong. Others claim to know Jesus as a person; yet, when their experience is not backed up with correct doctrine, they too are wrong. Belief in Jesus Christ is finding the way that leads to Heaven. When you find it, you must do something about it. "That if thou shalt confess with thy mouth the Lord Jesus, and shalt believe in thine heart that God hath raised him from the dead, thou shalt be saved" (Romans 10:9). You respond by belief in the heart and a confession of the mouth.

SALVATION—A TOTAL EXPERIENCE

Belief is not head knowledge only. It involves a total response to God. When you get on a jet liner, you can't place only one leg on the plane and fly to another city. You must respond completely by placing yourself wholly in the plane. Salvation is the same total experience. You must put your complete trust in Jesus Christ, trusting Him to take you to Heaven. This involves your intellect, emotion, and will.

1. *Using the intellect is the first step of experience.* A person must know God's plan of salvation before he can accept it. Just as you cannot communicate to another person apart from understanding, God follows the same law: God cannot communicate with you unless you understand His plan of salvation.

Knowledge involves awareness and understanding, but knowledge does not convert the soul. Jesus illustrates this point: "Not every one that saith unto me, Lord, Lord, shall enter into the kingdom of heaven; but he that doeth the will of my Father which is in heaven" (Matthew 7:21). These people had knowledge but it did little good. Jesus said, "I never knew you" (Matthew 7:23), even though they had head knowledge of the Lord.

2. *The stirring of emotions is the second step of experience.* Man is an emotional being. He feels deeply about many issues. We cannot neglect the part emotion plays in conversion, although not everyone will express it openly. Some clap their hands and sing for joy. Others weep and agonize. On the other hand, some are converted without any outward display of emotions.

A man in Roanoke, Virginia confessed to his wife that he had committed adultery. In a blinding rage, she ripped the curtains from the window, broke all the dishes and announced she was suing for divorce. The next Sunday morning the couple attended church and, during the invitation, he went forward, crying like a brokenhearted lover. A few minutes later she followed him to the altar. After the service was over, those who stood around were embarrassed by their hugs and kisses. Theirs was an emotional salvation—emotional both before and after receiving Christ.

Dr. Curtis Hutson, evangelist and former pastor of Forrest Hills Baptist Church, Decatur, Georgia visited in the home of Cleo Jenkins, a Certified Public Accountant. After analyzing the gospel, Cleo received the Lord. Later Hutson confessed, "I didn't think he was saved because he didn't show any feelings." Yet Cleo has gone on to become one of the greatest workers in the church.

What place do emotions have in conversion? We should never judge a man's seriousness by his tears at the altar. Felix trembled and answered, "Go thy way for this time; when I have a convenient season, I will call for thee" (Acts 24:25).

His emotions were stirred, just as some who come to the altar and weep yet never are saved. We cannot judge the sincerity of a person by the outward display of emotions. The country preacher said it eloquently, "The toot of the car's horn doesn't tell you how much gas is in the tank."

On the other side of the coin, because a person does not cry or show joy doesn't mean he lacks sincerity. Many people keep their emotions to themselves, yet they feel deeply.

Just as knowledge alone cannot save, so religious emotionalism will not get a man to Heaven. God uses emotions to motivate a man to seek relief. Some are terrified of judgment and seek salvation. Others are overwhelmed with love. Other emotions which might make a person seek salvation are guilt, gratitude, pressure, or uncertainty.

Emotions, like repentance, are an outward manifestation of an inner work of God. After a person is saved, he might experience feelings of relief, joy, or tears of happiness.

3. *The response of the will is the third step of experience.* There is nothing a person can do to save himself—Jesus Christ has done it all. But a man must respond with his inner being: he must accept salvation.

Faith is believing in Jesus Christ. You know what the Bible says He did for you on the cross and you accept it. Your feelings are stirred by the convicting work of the Holy Spirit and you respond by an act of the will. You have expressed Biblical faith.

When man's will responds in belief, it is an act of obedience to God. "But ye have obeyed from the heart that form of doctrine which was delivered you" (Romans 6:17). The will must say yes to God.

Repentance is necessary for salvation, but repentance does not save one. Like the bus ticket which says, "This half good for passage, not good if detached," salvation is good for passage to Heaven, but salvation is not salvation if detached from repentance. The second half of the bus ticket reads, "Not good for passage; keep in your possession until arriving at destination." This ticket stub represents repentance: Not good for passage to Heaven; keep doing good works until you get to your destination.

Eternal life does not begin with repentance for these are dead works that cannot merit you before God. Your eternal life begins when Christ comes into your heart. The Bible gives life. When you hear the preaching of the gospel, it is God's Word that stirs the heart.

Conviction which stirs the spirit to respond to God begins with the Scriptures: "For the word of God is quick, and powerful . . . and is a discerner of the thoughts and intents of the heart" (Hebrews 4:12). The Word of God lays bare the sin that is hidden in the thoughts of man. Our sin is never hidden from God but the Bible convicts us by illuminating the mind, showing us our sinfulness.

Conviction begins deep in the mind and moves to consciousness. A man becomes aware that he has offended God. The effect is that he cries, trembles, or becomes reflective. Sad stories or persuasive arguments will not bring conviction. It comes from the Word of God by the Holy Spirit. The Holy Spirit convicted you of sin (John 16:8) because you had not believed in Jesus Christ (John 16:9). He also performed the same work of conviction in your heart concerning righteousness and judgment (John 16:8-10).

Tears will not convince God of your sincerity, nor will your smile convince others that you have an inner peace. The stirring of the emotions is a necessary concomitant of salvation, not salvation itself. You must respond.

Your mind knows the facts of the gospel and your emotions motivate you, but your will must respond. Paul describes this: ". . . Ye have obeyed from the heart that form of doctrine . . ." (Romans 6:17). Other descriptions are used to show this response: receiving Christ, accepting the Lord, asking Christ into your heart, placing your trust in Christ, or taking Christ by faith. Each of these statements means a person has made a volitional act of his will in turning his life over to Jesus Christ.

A young man was dealing for the first time with a seeker at the church altar. He told the person to pray, "Dear Jesus, come into my heart. . . ." When they got up, the soul-winner thought of an extra prayer. They returned to the altar where he instructed the seeker to pray, "Dear Jesus, forgive me of my sins . . . ."

As they returned to the first pew, he thought of a third prayer, "Dear Jesus, take me to Heaven . . . ." Actually, people are saved by using any one of the three formulas. God is not as interested in the words of your mouth as He is in the attitude of your heart.

So, to be truly saved, you must *know the content* of the gospel, *respond by your emotions,* and make a *decision of your will* to turn your life over to Christ.

Chapter 2
What God Did to Save You

What does it take to get a person ready for Heaven? If you listen to several churches you will hear them tell you: be baptized, come to Bible classes, go forward, take communion, and/or quit smoking cigarettes. None of these instructions will forgive your sins. You must meet God in a real way if you want to go to Heaven.

A nine-year-old boy visited the Buffalo Avenue Baptist Church, Tampa, Florida. When the teacher picked up the roll book, he asked the boy's name.

"Bobby Gray."

"Are you saved?" the teacher asked the scared boy.

"No."

"Do you want to become a Christian?" the teacher asked. When the boy said yes, the teacher pulled his chair next to Bobby's and read the plan of salvation. The other boys listened.

"Let's get on our knees and you accept Christ," the gentle teacher instructed. All the boys in the class knelt on the rough concrete. They heard Bobby Gray pray, repeating the prayer directed by the teacher.

"Dear Jesus, please come into my heart and save me. I am sorry for my sin; forgive me and make me ready for Heaven."

Some might question if the nine-year-old boy could be changed for eternity by a short prayer like that. The teacher told me the story and confessed, "That was the first person I ever led to the Lord. It was so simple and unemotional that I wondered if the boy really was saved."

There is no doubt in anyone's mind today because that boy became Dr. Bob Gray, pastor of Trinity Baptist Church, Jacksonville, Florida, the tenth largest church in the United States.

Bobby Gray came to the Lord, but behind the scenes God was working to save him. First, God worked in his heart; and, second, God worked at Calvary. God follows this same pattern for everyone who is saved.

GOD WORKS IN THE HEART

1. *God motivated someone to give you the gospel.* Hearing the gospel is important because the Bible promises: ". . . faith cometh by hearing, and hearing by the word of God" (Romans 10:17). You may have heard the gospel from one person or from many persons. You may have heard it in a sermon, Bible study, or from a soul-winner. You may have heard it once or many times. Paul wrote, "How beautiful are the feet of them that preach the gospel of peace, and bring glad tidings of good things!" (Romans 10:15).

Are you thankful for those who were concerned enough about you to tell you of God's plan of salvation? The gospel is the good news that Jesus died for your sins (I Corinthians 15:1-3). But just hearing the gospel is not enough to save a person. Some have a false security, thinking they have salvation because they have heard it. Jesus said: ". . . By hearing ye shall hear, and shall not understand . . ." (Matthew 13:14). Hearing is only the first step.

2. *God planted the Bible as a seed in your heart.* God has a tool for your salvation; it is the Bible. "Being born again . . . by the word of God, which liveth and abideth for ever" (I Peter 1:23). Because the Bible produces salvation, it is more than a record of sacred history. The Bible is a living book (Hebrews 4:12). When the Bible was planted in your heart, like a seed it grew and sprouted into life. The Bible produces eternal life.

How can the Bible give life? The answer is found in the way the Word of God was written. Its origin and content are not like any other book. The Bible is inspired (I Timothy 3:16), meaning it was written by God. The Holy Spirit breathed life into its authors who wrote the Word of God so that their words came directly from God, not man. Since God is life, when His Word is planted into our hearts, it produces life.

There is a second step in the life-giving properties of the Bible. Its message is different; there is a unique message in the pages of Scripture. It says that man has sinned against God and will be punished for his rebellion. But the Bible does not end with that dismal picture. It announces that Jesus Christ has died for the sins of the world, and they that believe in Him will not perish but have everlasting life (John 3:16,36). When you believe God's message, you gain eternal life. Just as life begins with birth, so eternal life begins when you are born again.

Drunks have read the Bible and permanently sobered up because they were born again. Rebellious teenagers have heard the Bible in a youth rally and learned submission because they were born again. Small children have memorized Scripture in Sunday School and lived their entire lives for God because they were born again.

The Word of God is likened to seed in Mark 4:14. It grows when planted in the human heart. The seed germinates under the soil before breaking into the sunlight. The Bible has the same effect in our heart. Some are converted immediately upon hearing the Word of God. Others hear the Bible many hours before they are converted. But in the time prior to their conversion, the Bible is working in their hearts. It gives knowledge of sin, producing guilt and conviction (John 16:7-11). Sometimes conviction is manifested with tears (II Corinthians 7:9-10); at other times people silently respond.

3. *God brought conviction for your sins.* God is continually seeking out those who should be saved and calling them to Himself. He uses the Holy Spirit to bring people to Christ. God brings a man to salvation by convicting him of his sins. This draws or motivates the sinner to Christ; "No man can come to me," Jesus said, "except the Father which hath sent me draw him" (John 6:44). Conviction makes a man uneasy about his sin.

When conviction hits one man, he may be sorry for cursing. The next man is afraid of going to Hell. A third man will feel ashamed to stand in the presence of a holy God. The Holy Spirit reveals sin in the heart like an inspector crawling in a dark, dirty engine room with a flashlight looking for trouble.

The Holy Spirit and sin conflict like boxers in the ring. Both struggle for mastery of your heart. Some people will quit going to church to get away from the unpleasant feeling of conviction. Conviction unsettles the personality.

The body struggles with a high fever or nasal congestion when it has a virus; only rest will cure the common cold. Just so, the soul struggles under conviction and only the rest of salvation will cure its problem. The time you were under conviction may have been very difficult but it was a blessing because it brought you to the place of repentance.

Jesus said we are born of the water and of the Spirit (John 3:5). Water is a picture of the Word of God (Ephesians 5:26), the instrument of salvation. The Holy Spirit is the agent that works in the heart to produce the born-again experience. The Holy Spirit works in our hearts before conversion to bring conviction. He works upon the Word of God that has been planted in the heart. The seeker may read the Bible. At other times, a soul-winner or preacher will give him the Word of God.

However it is done, the Holy Spirit illuminates the mind to understand the Bible. Understanding brings conviction. God puts pressure on the person to respond to Jesus Christ. Even when a man is searching for God, it is the Holy Spirit who is seeking him out. As the mountaineer said, "I chased the Lord till He caught me."

There are nine important, formative months after conception before a baby is born. But the final act of birth is equally important. The time of birth is recorded by the hospital. Even though the baby has been in the process of life for nine months, the segment of time in which the birth occurs is vital. It is the final product that is important. If the baby is not born healthy, nine months of preparation were futile.

Nine months are not necessary for a person's spiritual conversion. It may happen quickly the first time one hears the gospel, or it may be stretched out over a lengthy time. Some people run from God for years, even decades. Some hear the gospel in their teen years but aren't saved until adulthood. But even when they were running from God, the Scriptures and the Holy Spirit were at work in their hearts. The Bible is called a fire that burns in the heart (Jeremiah 20:9), and the Holy Spirit is pictured as one who strives with men (Genesis 6:3).

Just as a baby is born at a specific hour in a designated place, so is conversion. You do not grow into salvation. You must make a decision for Christ at some point in time.

On the Day of Pentecost approximately 3,000 people believed and were baptized. That was the day of their spiritual birth. The Philippian jailer was told in the middle of the night, "Believe on the Lord Jesus Christ, and thou shalt be saved . . ." (Acts 16:31). That night he became a Christian and was baptized.

You are born again when you ask Jesus Christ to come into your heart. "But as many as received him [Jesus], to them gave he power to become the sons of God . . . which were born, not of blood, nor of the will of the flesh, nor of the will of man, but of God" (John 1:12-13).

We have discussed what God did in your heart; this is only half of the picture. The first half is man-centered; the second half is what Christ accomplished for you.

WHAT GOD DID AT CALVARY

God gave His only begotten Son to die on the cross of Calvary in your place because of your sin. In dying Christ simultaneously accomplished many things on the cross for us. All of these applied instantaneously the moment we were saved. This once-for-all act of history is the basis for our salvation experience. Don't ever let Satan convince you otherwise.

1. *God cleansed you of all your sins by the blood of Christ.* Hebrews 9:22 tells us that ". . . without shedding of blood is no remission [of sin]." The life of a creature is

in its blood (Deuteronomy 12:23). When Jesus shed His blood, He gave His life. He gave Himself as a substitute for sin. Jesus became a man in order to have a body which could be offered up as the only worthy sacrifice for the sins of men. He was born without sin and lived without sin. He was perfect. We were sinners, failures in God's sight.

God accepted Christ's blood for our sin. If you are caught speeding, you have to pay a fine. Your money is the price for breaking the law. You are free to leave the judge's courtroom because the price was paid. The blood of Christ is the price that forgives your sin (I Peter 1:18,19). Now you can leave God's courtroom a free person.

2. *You were justified and made perfect before God.* Before you were saved, you were alienated from God. You may have been an average citizen without filthy habits. Or you may have committed every crime in the book. But no person, no matter how good or bad, can reach God without help.

The United States cannot help citizens of Russia because they belong to another government. When an alien becomes a United States citizen, he can claim the benefits guaranteed under the Constitution and Bill of Rights. Likewise, as an alien, you could not claim the benefits of Heaven. But when you put your faith in Christ, God changed your citizenship. Now you belong to a new nation: you have a new King. This is the act of *justification.*

Paul wrote, "Therefore being justified by faith, we have peace with God through our Lord Jesus Christ." He went on to write, "For if, when we were enemies, we were reconciled to God by the death of his Son, much more, being reconciled, we shall be saved by his life" (Romans 5:1,10).

When you are justified, God declares you righteous, just as if you had never sinned. When a man goes to prison, his record shows he is a criminal; his confinement shows he is a criminal. A pardon gets him out of prison and forgives his crime, but his record shows he is an ex-con.

In a similar picture, the forgiveness of sins gets a man out of Hell, but he is still an ex-sinner. Justification makes his record perfect. He is no longer an ex-sinner, but made just-as-if-he'd-never-sinned. The sinner becomes as perfect as God's Son. Justification equips a man for Heaven as though he had never sinned once.

Now that you are saved you want to learn how to live the successful Christian life. That is now possible since God has adjusted your record in Heaven to appear as if you have never sinned. Try to live according to your record.

3. *God made you His child.* All men are "children of God" by creation, but that is not good enough for claiming salvation. The Bible claims we were also children of Satan (John 8:44) and of disobedience (Ephesians 2:2). We could not rightfully pray, ". . . Our Father which art in Heaven . . ." (Matthew 6:9) without salvation.

Salvation is described as being born again (John 3:7). You were born into God's family. You became a child of God by receiving Jesus Christ as your Saviour. "But as many as received him, to them gave he power to become the sons of God" (John 1:12). Perhaps you went forward to the altar; there you prayed, "Come into my heart and save me." If you were sincere, you became a child of God; now you can call God your Father.

In one sense, God is the Lord to be reverenced because He judges sin and demands righteousness. The Bible says God is a consuming fire (Hebrews 12:29). You should never take your relationship with God lightly. But on the other hand, you can be intimate with God because He is your Heavenly Father. Just as a child runs into his father's arms, you can go to God in prayer. He will never turn you away. When Christ came into your heart, you became worthy to approach God. You have His nature (II Peter 1:4); you belong to Him.

4. *God gave you a new nature which means you have a new life.* Paul referred to sinners as being "dead in trespasses and sins" (Ephesians 2:1). He knew sinners were alive physically, mentally, and emotionally, but they were dead spiritually. Your spirit, which is capable of knowing God, was dormant and inoperative until it was made alive in Christ. "Therefore if any man be in Christ, he is a new creature: old things are passed away; behold, all things are become new" (II Corinthians 5:17). Only after the new birth can a person grow spiritually.

The new nature opens many wonderful vistas to you. Before you were saved you probably didn't want to pray, listen to sermons, or win souls. Before you were saved you might have craved drink, evil friends, and enjoyed evil thoughts.

Now you should have experienced a "flip-flop" in attitude. You should have new friends. Things about the church you previously thought were silly should have become meaningful. You should want to pray and study the Bible. You should become embarrassed by your temper and uncontrolled desires. Your new nature should change your life.

To be a successful Christian, you must let the new nature control you. You are to "put off concerning the former conversation the old man . . ." (Ephesians 4:22). Don't allow the things which controlled you before salvation to control you now. At the same time, you are to "put on the new man, which after God is created in righteousness" (Ephesians 4:24). God has given you a new nature; you are responsible to let it direct you into success.

5. *God put His seal of ownership upon you through the ministry of the Holy Spirit.* When you became a Christian, you no longer belonged to yourself; you belonged to God. Ephesians 1:13 says that "after that ye believed, ye were sealed with that holy Spirit of promise." Ephesians 1:14 goes on to say that the presence of the Holy Spirit in the believer "is the earnest of our inheritance until the redemption of the purchased possession, unto the praise of his glory."

God has marked us with His seal. Ford automobiles have a "Ford" trademark stamped into the engine block. In the same way, God stamps His children. The same idea is continued in II Corinthians 1:22 which states that God "hath also sealed us, and given the earnest of the Spirit in our hearts."

WHAT EVIDENCES GOD EXPECTS

The salvation experience is not the end of God's dealings with you, but the beginning of a whole new relationship. Christians are expected to "grow in grace, and in the knowledge of our Lord and Saviour Jesus Christ" (II Peter 3:18). Here are some of the things for which they are responsible.

1. *There is the matter of restitution.* If you wronged other people before you were saved, you ought to go to them and make things right. Making restitution may be impossible in some cases if you don't know how to contact them or if they have died, but if possible restitution should be made.

Acts of restitution should be done quietly and without publicity. This can be a wonderful way to testify of what Christ has done for you. It may involve humbling and embarrassing situations, but don't let this discourage you. If there are people you offended who will not forgive you, you just have to leave their situations with God and go on from there.

Perhaps the best Biblical example of a believer making restitution is that of little Zacchaeus in Jericho. Jesus invited Himself to the home of this hated tax collector. Evidently Jesus made a great influence on Zacchaeus because he said, "Behold, Lord, the half of my goods I give to the poor; and if I have taken any thing from any man by false accusation, I restore him fourfold." Jesus was so impressed by his promise that He observed, "This day is salvation come to this house" (Luke 19:8,9).

2. *There is the matter of identifying with Christ.* A new convert should try to live as much like Christ as possible. Several things are involved.

The convert should be baptized immediately, an outward act showing an inner change. In the early church, baptism took place as soon after conversion as possible. Baptism is your identification with Christ in His death, burial, and resurrection and your identification with a local church through being placed into the local body of Christ.

You should attend all the services of your church to fellowship with other Christians for mutual encouragement and service. "And let us consider one another to provoke [or stimulate] unto love and to good works: Not forsaking the assembling of ourselves together, as the manner of some is; but exhorting one another: and so much the more, as ye see the day [of Christ's return] approaching" (Hebrews 10:24-25).

You should immediately tell someone that you are saved. Then follow the example of Christ in telling others the good news of salvation. Jesus said, "Whosoever therefore shall confess me before men, him will I confess also before my Father which is in heaven" (Matthew

10:32).

You should be willing to share in the sufferings of Christ. There may be persecutions now that you are saved. Realizing that Jesus had suffered to make salvation for men possible, Paul felt he had a responsibility to fulfill his own share of suffering in getting the gospel message out to lost men (Colossians 1:24,25). He also was willing to suffer for Jesus if it meant that he could know the same kind of power in his life which Christ had experienced when He was raised from the grave (Philippians 3:10-11).

You should make regular use of the means of grace which God has provided for spiritual growth. These include prayer, Bible reading, and study.

3. *There is the matter of keeping yourself separated from the world system.* "Be ye not unequally yoked together with unbelievers: for what fellowship hath righteousness with unrighteousness? and what communion hath light with darkness? . . . Wherefore come out from among them, and be ye separate, saith the Lord, and touch not the unclean thing; and I will receive you, And will be a Father unto you, and ye shall be my sons and daughters, saith the Lord Almighty" (II Corinthians 6:14,17,18).

Now that you are a born-again believer, it is a good idea to remind yourself often of what Christ did for you at Calvary. If doubts come and you question your feelings about salvation, recall the fact that Christ died for you. Accept that atonement and realize you were made a new creation in Him (Romans 5:17). Satan will try to defeat you, but you need not be ignorant of his devices (II Corinthians 2:11). Nothing can separate you from Him and His love (Romans 8:35-39).

PART II

Getting Started Right in the Christian Life

Chapter 3
Be Sure of Your Salvation

One of the first obstacles you will face in your Christian life is doubts. You may have many doubts but none is so demoralizing as doubting your salvation.

Jim Carlson was a Christian businessman in Atlanta, Georgia. He sat across the desk from his pastor and with difficulty said, "I'm not sure God loves me. The Lord did not hear my prayer." His wife had died of cancer, leaving him with two daughters.

"I asked God to heal her and He didn't," continued the young salesman. "When she suffered, I asked God to take her and He didn't do *that* immediately." Jim explained that he was $45,000 in debt due to a $300 a day hospital bill, plus doctor's fees. He didn't have money for a babysitter and had filed for bankruptcy.

"How can God do this to me?" was his question.

If ever a man's works demonstrated his salvation, Jim Carlson's had. He had taught Sunday School, held family altar, and was respected at the office for his testimony. But now he was confused. Difficult circumstances had clouded his relationship with God. But Jim rebounded and served God once again.

You may have doubts about your salvation when you pray and the Heavens seem shut up. Circumstances may one day make you doubt you are a Christian, even though you are presently confident of the fact. This chapter is written to give reasons for the assurance of your salvation.

Sometimes Christians have doubts when their circumstances are not nearly as spectacular as Jim's. A middle-aged housewife came forward during an invitation to confess her sin of depression. "How can I be a Christian and stay so miserable?" She doubted her salvation because of her depression.

A teenage boy stood chatting with some friends. Someone told a story and when the punch line came, it was dirty. The teenage boy laughed, but inwardly he thought, "Christians shouldn't laugh at dirty stories. Am I really a Christian?" While riding his motorcycle down the street, a young man saw a girl sunbathing in a bikini on her front lawn. He looked two or three times, then thought to himself, "I shouldn't be doing this. Am I a Christian?" He doubted his salvation because of temptation.

Others have doubts because they are ignorant of the Scriptures. An unchurched mother was invited to a Bible study where she began learning the Word of God. Many of her questions were answered. Later she attended an evangelistic service, went forward during the invitation, and had a deep experience with Christ. Her life was turned around.

All the way home she sang the hymns she had learned. She threw her arms around her husband, saying, "Honey, I got saved." She gathered the family together and told them the thrilling story. A week later she broke her leg on the back steps. Her housework piled up, the kids fought when they took care of the chores, and she got discouraged. The height of her salvation became the depth of despondency.

"Was it real?" she wondered. She had let her emotions prop up her Christian life to the point where she depended on them.

Others have doubts for a different reason. After I spoke at the Philadelphia Sunday School Convention, I gave an invitation for teachers to come forward and dedicate themselves to double their class attendance. A middle-aged lady had come to the civic center meeting by mistake. But she felt a need and had come forward at the end of my message.

"Something is wrong with my spiritual life," she kept telling me. She had previously come forward during a giant crusade in the same arena.

"Did you ask Christ to come into your heart?" I asked. She answered, "Yes." But she was not praying, reading her Bible, nor had she attended church.

"I don't even want to," she answered. "I thought going forward was just emotion, so I dismissed it from my mind until tonight. I choked up just like I did two years ago."

After talking with her for 30 minutes, I determined she had not been saved. I realized she had only voiced a few words the previous time. She prayed the sinner's prayer, then we talked about how she should grow spiritually. Later I received a letter telling me, "I feel it all the time."

This lady had doubted because she was not saved. Too many people depend upon their feeling saved and not upon the basis of their salvation. They want to add to their salvation experience their ability to "stick it out" as a requirement for getting to Heaven. And when they fail, as they surely will at times, they believe they have to get saved again almost every time there is a revival meeting.

What they need is an assurance of salvation, the knowledge that believers are saved—absolutely, perfectly, eternally saved. There is no such thing as partly saved and partly lost, partly justified and partly guilty, partly alive and partly dead, partly born of God and partly not. You become a believer through the experience of salvation based on the finished work of Christ on the cross for you. And your salvation is secure throughout all eternity.

Your condition may be similar to this woman's, with nagging doubts about your spiritual condition. You may have doubts about your salvation and, when you compare your circumstances to the checklist which follows, you may realize you are lost. This thought is not intended to unsettle you, but to help you find out the truth about your spiritual condition.

THE BASIS OF YOUR ASSURANCE

"There is nothing sure in life but death and taxes," the saying goes. But that is not true. You can be sure of your salvation. Just as you are sure that you will go down when falling from a tree, you can know that God has saved your soul. Just as you know that a fire is certainly hot, you can know that you have eternal life. This is called the assurance of salvation. It is the opposite of doubt, and it is based on Scriptural facts.

1. *Assurance of salvation comes because you have Christ in your heart.* First John 5:12 states clearly, "He that hath the Son hath life . . . ." Jesus Christ came into your heart when you invited Him in. If you have the Saviour, you are saved. Christ says in Revelation 3:20,

"Behold, I stand at the door, and knock: if any man hear my voice, and open the door, I will come in . . . ." With His entrance comes eternal life. "Christ in you, the hope of glory" (Colossians 1:27).

I started attending revival services when I was a seventeen-year-old teenager. The pastor realized I didn't know I was lost. I was trusting in my church membership. I was not convinced I needed to be saved. The pastor took me on a hospital visit.

"Go, lead everyone in that ward to Christ," he said. I began passing out tracts.

An elderly man asked me, "How do you get to Heaven?" The only answer I could give was an erroneous one I had been taught.

"Believe in Christ and do the best you can," I told the old gentleman.

"I don't think you are correct," the man replied. "You might not have salvation either."

The seed of concern was planted in my heart. It grew after I went to a church prayer meeting where people gave testimony of having Christ in their hearts. I returned home and knelt by my bed and prayed, "Lord, I don't think I have ever done it before, but I want Christ in my heart now." I experienced salvation when Christ came into my heart.

2. *Assurance of salvation comes from the witness of the Word of God.* "He that believeth on the Son of God hath the witness in himself" (I John 5:10). *Hath* means you have salvation—now. It does not say, "He that belongs to a church. . . ." It is not a question of who is right, but of what the Bible says. "And this is the record, that God hath given to us eternal life, and this life is in his Son" (I John 5:11).

Whereas the first reason dealt with experience, this proof of salvation is based in the facts of the Bible. If you have received Christ, you should not have doubts about your salvation, because God promised to save those who trust in Him. If you want assurance, first study the Bible promises of salvation, then claim them. God never goes back on His promises, so the promises provide anchors which hold the believer fast.

Certain verses in the Bible make the offer of salvation crystal clear. These should remove any doubts you have about your relationship with God. "For God so loved the world, that he gave his only begotten Son, that whosoever believeth in him should not perish, but have everlasting life" (John 3:16). "Believe on the Lord Jesus Christ, and thou shalt be saved, and thy house" (Acts 16:31). "If thou shalt confess with thy mouth the Lord Jesus, and shalt believe in thine heart that God hath raised him from the dead, thou shalt be saved" (Romans 10:9). Assurance is based on accepting these promises and acting upon them.

Paul had much to say about assurance. He wrote that the gospel came to believers "in power, and in the Holy Ghost, and in much assurance . . ." (I Thessalonians 1:5). He told believers that he was "confident of this very thing, that he which hath begun a good work in you will perform it until the day of Jesus Christ" (Philippians 1:6). Paul's own personal testimony was, "I know whom I have believed, and am persuaded that he is able to keep that which I have committed unto him against that day" (II Timothy 1:12).

The writer of Hebrews expressed his desire that believers enjoy full assurance of their hope to the end (Hebrews 6:11). He rejoiced in the fact that Christ had opened the way for men to approach God, "Having an high priest over the house of God; Let us draw near with a true heart in full assurance of faith" (Hebrews 10:21-22).

The Apostle John said believers could assure themselves of a right relationship with God by keeping His commandments (I John 2:3; 3:22). He said believers can *know* they have eternal life by studying Scriptural truth (I John 5:13).

Jude said that believers are preserved in Christ (Jude 1), that God is able to keep them from falling and will receive them into His presence as if they were faultless, because of their identification with their Saviour (Jude 24-25).

The promises of God guarantee our security. The Bible asks, "Who shall separate us from the love of Christ?" (Romans 8:35). The answer is obvious—nothing.

3. *Assurance of salvation comes because God answers your prayers.* The Lord has promised to answer the prayers of His children. "If ye shall ask any thing in my name, I will do it" (John 14:14). Of course, there are conditions to prayer, but when you meet these conditions, God will answer your prayers.

On the other hand, God has stated that He will not answer the prayers of the unsaved. "Behold, the Lord's hand is not shortened, that it cannot save; neither his ear heavy, that it cannot hear: But your iniquities have separated between you and your God, and your sins have hid his face from you, that he will not hear" (Isaiah 59:1,2). Also see John 9:31, 14:14; 15:7; Matthew 7:7,8; and I John 5:14,15. "If I regard iniquity in my heart, the Lord will not hear me" (Psalm 66:18). The only prayer God can answer for the unsaved is, "God be merciful to me, a sinner, and save me for Jesus' sake."

"And this is the confidence that we have in him, that, if we ask any thing according to his will, he heareth us: And if we know that he hear us, whatsoever we ask, we know that we have the petitions that we desired of him" (I John 5:14,15).

4. *Assurance of salvation comes if you understand the Bible.* John promises, "And we know that the Son of God is come, and hath given us an understanding . . ." (I John 5:20). An inner understanding of the Bible is proof that you are a Christian. Why? Because unsaved people are blinded to spiritual truths. "But the natural man receiveth not the things of the Spirit of God" (I Corinthians 2:14). This is again described by Paul as "having the understanding darkened" (Ephesians 4:18).

Just as a blind man cannot see the world about him, the unsaved man is blind to God's Word; he cannot understand the message of the Bible. He knows the meaning of words and the plot of a story, but the spiritual message of redemption is withheld from him.

Before you were saved, the Holy Spirit convicted you of sin, righteousness, and judgment (John 16:9-11). The word *convict* means to cause to see; the Holy Spirit made you see or understand God's plan of redemption. This was the work of God in your heart, bringing you to salvation. Those who rejected were further blinded. Now, if you have a desire to read the Bible and understand God's message, you are saved. This does not mean you could pass a test in Biblical knowledge, but you understand the plan of salvation.

5. *Assurance of salvation comes when you want to keep His commandments.* God's commandments are based on His nature; they are what He wants us to do. The natural man has a sinful nature and doesn't want to follow God. When you were unsaved, you did not want to do God's will. However, after you received Christ, there came a desire to do God's will (II Corinthians 5:17), even if you didn't always follow your desire.

A young father put off receiving Christ for several months. The pastor went by to talk with him on several occasions but the father always said, "Later." Finally he told the pastor that he came from a family that had always had beer and wine with their meals. "When I go back home for a family reunion, I know I'll drink alcohol with them."

The pastor showed him the victory that was promised in Jesus Christ, and the young father was saved. A year later, he came to the altar one Sunday morning, crying. He wouldn't let anyone deal with him but the pastor.

"I have been drinking with some buddies. I must not be saved." The pastor prayed for wisdom in handling the situation.

"Do you remember drinking wine with your family on New Year's Day right before you got saved?" the pastor asked the young man.

"Yes," he replied.

"And do you remember drinking on Christmas right before that?" Again he said yes. The pastor pointed out that the young man did not feel convicted at that time, did not show emotional upheaval and tears.

"Why are you crying over your drinking now?" the pastor asked. The father saw the point. Christ lived in his heart so he could no longer go back to his old habits without offending Jesus Christ.

Assurance of salvation comes when you realize you have new desires. "We know that whosoever is born of God sinneth not; but he that is begotten of God keepeth himself, and that wicked one toucheth him not" (I John 5:18). This sounds like a contradiction of I John 1:8: "If we say that we have no sin, we deceive ourselves, and the truth is not in us." One verse says a Christian will sin; the other says a Christian will not sin. What is the answer?

The second verse indicates the Christian still has a sinful *nature.* First John 1:10 states, "If we say that we have not sinned, we make him a liar, and his word is not in us." The verse, "Whosoever is born of God sinneth not"

(I John 5:18), describes the Christian's new nature. Your new nature cannot sin; it wants to do the will of God.

"Whosoever is born of God sinneth not" has been wrongly used to prove sinless perfection. The original language indicates *sinneth not* means "sinneth not continually." The Christian will not continue in sin, live there habitually. God puts the desire within him to live above sin.

A missionary to China told the story of a servant girl who worked in their home. Before the girl became a Christian, the missionary could not trust the girl because she stole articles around the home. It was necessary to search her before she left each day.

After she accepted Christ, while dusting one day the girl took a twenty dollar gold piece. But she came back in the middle of the night to return the stolen piece. Her new nature had made her miserable in her sin. If you are miserable in your sin, it is evidence of salvation.

Some go forward in church and make an open profession of faith, but there is no work in the heart. There is only an outward display. You can take a pig from the mud, scrub him and paste on lamb's wool so that he gives the appearance of being a sheep. But when you turn him out into the pasture, he will return to the mud with the pigs rather than eat grass with the sheep. It is the pig's nature. The Christian is different; now you have a new nature. You might sin, but you won't like it.

6. *Assurance of salvation comes when you love the brethren.* Another proof of your salvation is love for Christians. "We know that we have passed from death unto life, because we love the brethren. He that loveth not his brother abideth in death" (I John 3:14). Love manifests itself first in fellowship. When you are born again, you want to be around other Christians. Since God is Father to both you and other Christians, there is a com-

mon bond among you. Love manifests itself in a burden for other Christians. When you see a Christian sin and it bothers you, that is a sign you are saved. When you see a Christian with a need and you want to help him, that also is a sign that you are saved. When you see a victorious Christian and you want to live like him, rejoice, for your name is written in the Lamb's Book of Life.

A minister recently went to a mission church to preach for prayer meeting. The host pastor and his wife prepared a steak dinner with all the trimmings, including apple pie for dessert.

The crowd was small, only 26 present. The love offering for the guest preacher came to $26.00. When the visiting preacher discovered the financial pressures in the mission church and that the pastor only had a can of beans left in the cupboard, he gave him the $26.00. Both gave evidence of the fellowship of salvation; the mission pastor and his wife because they gave all except a can of beans, and the visiting pastor because he gave all in return.

Love of the brethren is proof of your salvation, but it does not mean you are not saved if you get mad at a Christian. Paul and Barnabas got angry at each other. Some Christians may do you wrong and you might lose your temper; this should not make you doubt your salvation.

If you like to fellowship with Christians at church, you are probably saved. If the people you love most in this world are Christians, you are probably saved. If they are not, you ought to ask yourself why.

Love is giving yourself to the one you love. When you give yourself to a group of Christians (the assembled church) and together you give yourselves to the Great Commission, you should have confidence that you are saved.

7. *Assurance of salvation comes when you have the inner witness of the Holy Spirit.* When you became a Christian, the Holy Spirit came into your heart to create a new nature within you (Romans 5:5) and to seal you until the final day of redemption (Ephesians 1:13-14). The Holy Spirit dwells in every Christian. One clue that a man is not saved is that he doesn't have the Holy Spirit (Romans 8:9).

The indwelling Holy Spirit witnesses that you are saved. He does not communicate through the ears or eyes. He communicates from His heart to your heart. "The Spirit itself beareth witness with our spirit, that we are the children of God" (Romans 8:16). This is innate knowledge, knowledge which doesn't need proof. Some young Christians, when asked how they know they are saved, reply, "I just know." They may not be educated or articulate, but they *know* they are saved. This is the witness of the Holy Spirit.

There are several New Testament references that show the Holy Spirit gives assurance. The Holy Spirit in our heart gives us assurance of sonship: "Because ye are sons, God hath sent forth the Spirit of his Son into your hearts, crying, Abba, Father" (Galatians 4:6). The Aramaic term *Abba* and the Greek term *Pater* are both used here. This means God is an intimate Father (papa).

The Apostle John said, "Hereby we know that he abideth in us, by the Spirit which he hath given us" (I John 3:24). He combined the concepts of the witness of the Spirit and belief in God's Word in I John 5:10: "He that believeth on the Son of God hath the witness in himself: he that believeth not God hath made him a liar; because he believeth not the record that God gave of his Son."

The inner presence of the Holy Spirit gives the desire to live a clean life. If you want to live a godly life, you are probably saved. Writing to believers, Paul said, "Being now made free from sin, and become servants to God, ye have your fruit unto holiness, and the end everlasting life" (Romans 6:22).

The best-known reference regarding the graces produced in the believer by the Holy Spirit is Galatians 5:22-23—"But the fruit of the Spirit is love, joy, peace, longsuffering, gentleness, goodness, faith, meekness, temperance: against such there is no law." If you are loving, joyful, peaceful, meek, and self-controlled, you will be fulfilling what the Holy Spirit desires for you. If you desire righteousness, you are probably saved.

Some Christians backslide; they don't desire a pure life. They don't portray what Paul wrote, "The fruit of the Spirit is [manifested] in all goodness and righteousness and truth" (Ephesians 5:9). We can't say the sinning saint is not saved. The Bible teaches that the child of God will sin, even though he shouldn't, and God has provided His way for the sinning Christian to be cleansed of his sin. Read I John 1:5-10 and realize that the apostle is writing to believers. But if a Christian does not follow this way of confessing his sin to God and being forgiven, God will chasten him.

The writer of Hebrews said divine discipline is administered to God's children. "No chastening for the present seemeth to be joyous, but grievous: nevertheless afterward it yieldeth the peaceable fruit of righteousness unto them which are exercised thereby [have been trained by it]" (Hebrews 12:11). If you have sinned and you realize you are suffering because of it, it is a sign that you are saved. If you get away with your sin, you might not be a child of God.

In summary then, these are the ways to know if you have been truly saved. You are saved if you believe God's Word and have applied the promises of salvation to yourself; you have the witness of the Spirit that you are a child of God; and you demonstrate the fruit of the Spirit in your life.

Don't let the enemy rob you of your assurance of salvation for God gave you these promises to hold you fast. It is a tragic thing for a believer to lack assurance; his spiritual life will stagnate. Doubt keeps him from the Bible, prayer, witnessing, and the desire to live for God. But once we become absolutely sure of our relationship to the Lord, our relationships with people will improve.

THE REWARDS OF ASSURANCE

Here are three of the main blessings you will enjoy from assurance.

1. *Your fear of being eternally lost is gone.* It is a terrible thing to constantly wonder whether your future destiny is Heaven or the Lake of Fire. A person lacking assurance is likely to become so discouraged that he gives up and begins to backslide. Or, he may become a legalist, thinking that by rigid adherence to a multitude of rules and regulations he can satisfy God and be saved in the end. Such actions are unfortunate and unnecessary.

2. *The assurance of your salvation will build your confidence in God.* When you read your Bible, you can accept and believe all its passages. When you pray, you can come to the throne of grace and find the help every believer has a right to expect from a loving and bountiful Heavenly Father. The time you once spent worrying about your position in Christ can now be devoted to service for Christ.

3. *When you are sure of your salvation, you will be able to witness to others better.* You can tell others that you have no doubt about having had your sins forgiven and you know where you will spend eternity. An invitation to another to accept Christ as personal Saviour must

be backed up by the conviction that you yourself think it is worthwhile.

Your search for assurance must find its conclusion in God. First, His Word provides the basis of salvation. Second, His Spirit provides the inner witness that speaks to your spirit. Finally, the fact of a changed life convinces you of salvation. Remember, the changed life is not self improvement; righteousness cannot be earned or self-induced. Your new nature must be imparted by God, and it will give assurance to those who put their faith in God and His Son, Jesus Christ.

Chapter 4
Become Grounded on the Word of God

As a Christian, the most indispensable instrument to your life is the Bible. You can't be Christian without it.

THE BIBLE TEACHES CHRISTIANS HOW TO LIVE

The first time Harold Shickley attended church he went forward and received Christ. The only things he knew about Christianity were the things he had heard on radio and television at Christmas and Easter.

"I don't know much about God," he told his pastor.

Harold was given a Bible and told to start reading it. "The Bible will keep you from sin . . . or sin will keep you from the Bible," his pastor told him.

"I don't understand it," he later told his pastor. As a matter of fact, he didn't understand much that happened the evening he was saved because it was his first time in church. But he knew in his heart something had happened to him.

Since Harold wasn't grounded in the principles of the faith he continued hanging around with his drinking buddies. At first he went to church, but gradually he lost the desire and drifted away.

"Why did you give up?" the pastor asked when they met in a convenience market.

"I just couldn't hold out," he replied.

"I'll help you grow in your faith," the pastor promised.

The defeated Harold agreed to "try" the Christian life again. This time the pastor showed him how to study the Bible. Harold began reading the Gospel of John. Staying up late at night, he devoured the pages of Scripture; like a hungry man he couldn't get enough. As the Bible changed his desires, his drinking buddies lost interest in him and he in them. The lesson was hard for Harold to learn, but the Word of God will keep a person from sin.

1. *You are protected from sin by the Word of God.* "Thy word have I hid in mine heart, that I might not sin against thee" (Psalm 119:11). The Bible keeps you from sin by its instructional power. It teaches the correct way of life. "Thy word is a lamp unto my feet, and a light unto my path" (Psalm 119:105). Historian Arnold Toynbee noted, "It pierces through the intellect and plays directly upon the heart."

The Scriptures are like a vaccination protecting you by cleansing your conscience (John 15:3); giving you joy (Jeremiah 15:16); correcting wrong teaching that would allow deviation (II Timothy 3:16); and producing a "hedge" against sin in your life (Hebrews 4:12).

2. *You grow in faith by the Word of God.* Five times the Bible refers to Christians as babes, and each time the

answer to immaturity is found in the Bible (I Corinthians 3:1-3; 4:14-21; Ephesians 4:14; Hebrews 5:11-14; I Peter 2:2). When you received Christ as Saviour, you were born into God's family. Now you must grow as a child of God.

There's nothing wrong with babies; in fact they are delightful. As a young father, I was first at the maternity ward each evening with a camera for pictures of Debbie. We kept a scrapbook with a record of her pounds, inches, and vital statistics. I bragged to Richard Strauss that my daughter would outgrow his son who was born at approximately the same time. If she had never grown, my expectations would have been destroyed.

Growth is the natural process of the foods we eat working in our bodies. If we eat the right things, we'll grow. A Christian must eat the right spiritual food to grow spiritually. Jeremiah noted, "Thy words were found, and I did eat them; and thy word was unto me the joy and rejoicing of mine heart" (Jeremiah 15:16). A man of God once told me that every reference to spiritual growth was connected with knowing and obeying the Bible, and he was right. If you don't eat properly, you eventually will get sick; and if you neglect the Word of God, you'll dry up spiritually like a shriveled raisin. The Bible is milk for the body (I Peter 2:2), meat for the growing Christian (Hebrews 5:12-14), bread for the hungry (John 6:51), and honey for satisfaction (Psalms 19:10).

3. *You hear the voice of God through the Word of God.* The Bible brings peace when your heart is troubled. For many years, the Gideons have placed Bibles in hotel rooms. Their files are filled with stories of men who have contemplated suicide, divorce, or an act of violence. Picking up the Bible, people have turned to the guide, "When in Trouble" and have found the Word of God gave them encouragement and hope.

The Christian hears the Bible with the ear of his heart.

God speaks to him through Scripture. Chiang Kai Shek testified, "The Bible is the voice of the Holy Spirit."

But what about the unsaved? What is his response to the Bible? First, the Scriptures work in one's heart to bring conviction. Paul describes Timothy's salvation: "And that from a child thou hast known the holy scriptures, which are able to make thee wise unto salvation through faith which is in Christ Jesus (II Timothy 3:15). Many children like young Timothy grow up in a Christian home, but it is the Scripture that brings them to Christ.

My sister Martha received Christ because she memorized the Word of God. She had her devotions "religiously" each night and never became involved in sin. Yet I felt she had not experienced salvation. I typed 100 verses on 3″ X 5″ cards and promised her a new Scofield Reference Bible when she could repeat them perfectly. As she quoted each verse, I instructed her in the verse's meaning. Halfway through the project, she went to camp. Phoning long distance, Martha told of conviction that led to salvation because an evangelist quoted the verses she had been learning.

But God's Word does more than speak to the innocent. It reaches the hardened heart, too. Two men struck up a conversation at an evangelistic crusade. Before the service both were critical of the evangelist's methods, but the speaker kept repeating the phrase, "The Bible says. . . ." At the invitation one man said to the other, "I don't know about you, but I'm going forward to get saved." The other hesitated a moment, then reached into his coat and replied, "Here's your wallet; I took it. I'll go with you."

4. *You will become successful through the Word of God.* There is no complete freedom although we hear many people today claim absolute liberty. Everyone, saved and unsaved, is responsible to God. As a lost per-

son you accepted Christ and fulfilled that responsibility to God. Now you must learn what God wants you to do and what He prohibits. The Bible is a guidebook containing both positive and negative principles which God expects you to follow. If you saturate yourself with scriptural principles, you will be able to live within His framework.

You become like Jesus Christ as you study the Bible. Paul tells us, "We all, with open face beholding as in a glass the glory of the Lord, are changed into the same image from glory to glory . . ." (II Corinthians 3:18). This verse illustrates a man standing before a mirror, which is God's Word. In the mirror he doesn't see his image, but a reflection of Jesus Christ. The more he studies the mirror (the Bible), the more he becomes like Jesus Christ.

Some habits will disappear immediately after conversion. Others will linger. The Bible is your source for overcoming all habits. As God's Word becomes a part of your thinking, you in turn will think like God and overcome bad habits.

THE BIBLE SHOULD BE STUDIED

The Bible is no ordinary book; it is inspired by God (II Timothy 3:16). Inspiration is not just a step higher than the creativity of Shakespeare, Tennyson or Mark Twain. The Bible is the Word of God. We must assume the attitudes of the Thessalonians: "When ye received the word of God which ye heard of us, ye received it not as the word of men, but as it is in truth, the word of God, which effectually worketh also in you that believe (I Thessalonians 2:13). When you study the Bible, you must not just study it as some other book. You must study it as God's Word.

The following principles for approaching the Word of God come from its pages: "These were more noble than those in Thessalonica, in that they received the word with all readiness of mind, and searched the scriptures daily, whether those things were so" (Acts 17:11).

1. *Study the Bible itself.* The Christians in Berea were titled "noble" because "they received the word with all readiness of mind, and searched the scriptures. . . ." Don't study books about the Bible first. These have their value, of course, but books are what *men* think about the Bible. Let the Holy Spirit speak directly to you. He can do it when you study the Scripture.

A young college student asked D. L. Moody's advice about his life's work after seminary.

"Don't go into business. Your father's wealthy and you have more money than you'll need. Devote your life to teaching the English Bible."

"I don't know it," was the astonished young man's reply.

"Don't you go to a religious college where they have professors to teach you the Bible?"

"Yes, that is true. But I have listened to one professor lecture for six months and we still haven't determined who wrote the first five books of the Bible."

Moody told the young man, "Study the Bible on your own; master its contents." The young man took his advice and became one of the greatest Bible teachers of his day. You, too, should begin studying the Bible so you can master its contents.

2. *Study the Bible diligently.* When you study the Bible, don't just casually read it, but drink in every word. The Berean Christians "searched the scriptures" (Acts 17:11). The word *searched* means investigated, inquired, sifted, or scrutinized.

Give attention to every word because God placed every word there for a reason. Get a dictionary and look up the important words. Get a Scofield Reference Bible and study the words in the reference column or in the subject index at the back of the book.

Try to remember everything you read. If your mind wanders, practice concentrating. You'll soon be able to concentrate on every verse.

"Tell me in one word how to study the Bible," a man once asked R. A. Torrey.

"That's not easy but if I could use only one word it would be *thoughtfully.*"

The Berean Christians "searched the scriptures daily, whether those things were so." They were not satisfied to just read the Bible; they wanted to know if the things Paul preached were accurate. A big mistake is made when we go to the Bible to fit our church's view into the verses we read.

3. *Study the entire Bible.* On Easter Sunday afternoon two disciples were walking to Emmaus. Jesus joined them, "And beginning at Moses and all the prophets, he expounded unto them in all the scriptures the things concerning himself" (Luke 24:27). In this short hike to Emmaus, Jesus covered the first five books of the Bible (Moses) through the last 17 books (all the prophets). Jesus evidently had studied all the Scripture. The fact that He taught it to His disciples shows He wants us to know it all, too.

Dr. Ash Moore, a missionary for fifty years, started teaching the Book of Hebrews. There were so many questions regarding the ceremonial law, he began teaching the book of Leviticus but still the questions came. He decided to go back to Genesis and start with the foundation of Scripture.

If you have never read through the Bible, do it now. Begin with Genesis. If you don't understand some things, don't get discouraged. Theodore Epp, speaker on "Back to the Bible," once said, "I had to read through the Bible ten times before I really understood it."

G. Campbell Morgan said one could read through the Bible at the pulpit rate in 60 hours. A banker challenged his statement.

"Well, sir, the proof lies with you," responded Morgan.

The banker returned to tell Morgan he was wrong. "I did it in 40 hours."

"I said the *pulpit rate,*" the wise old Morgan stroked his white beard. "You can't trust a banker's rate."

Some study a pet book such as John, Romans, Daniel or Revelation. Some study only pet subjects such as healing, dispensationalism, or the second coming. But the whole Bible is the Word of God; so we ought to study all of it.

4. *Study the Bible systematically.* Jesus must have studied the Bible as He taught it—systematically. ". . . Beginning at Moses and all the prophets, he expounded unto them in all the scriptures the things concerning himself" (Luke 24:27). In your study, pick a subject and follow it through. Take one word and look up every reference to that word in a concordance.

As you begin studying a book, go through it to the end. Dr. Curtis Hutson is a great doctrinal preacher, in spite of the fact that he never went to college. When asked where he had learned his doctrine, he answered, "What I know I've learned, one subject at a time, one book at a time." He went on to explain, "When I began studying a topic, I stayed with it until I got to the conclusion."

You should read through the Bible. Then go back and read each New Testament book through in one sitting. Finally, read the whole New Testament through in one weekend.

5. *Study the Bible as the Word of God that demands complete obedience to every command that applies to*

you. God will keep all the promises in the Bible. "All the promises of God in him are yea, and in him Amen . . ." (II Corinthians 1:20). God will keep all His promises because "It was [is] impossible for God to lie . . ." (Hebrews 6:18). When you study, you must trust God without reservation, doubt, or anxiety. The promises God made regarding His coming again to earth, He will keep. You cannot spiritualize these as His coming into your life. God will keep His promises, as He said—not as you want them fulfilled.

When the Bible promises something, believe it. When the feeble mind can't comprehend it, believe it. "In hope of eternal life, which God, that cannot lie, promised before the world began" (Titus 1:2).

While pastoring in Dallas, Texas, I was doing some carpenter work in the back of the auditorium. Gradually I felt self-conscious and turned around to see a small boy watching me. His presence changed my actions. When you study the Bible, visualize Christ standing there, speaking to you. The Bible will come alive as His presence changes your actions.

After I was engaged, my fiancee and I were separated for three summers. At mail call, I didn't dare read her letters in front of others. I'd go to my room, take out her picture and read the letter in privacy, pouring over every word. When you study the Bible, find a private place and picture Christ standing near.

6. *Study the Bible in an attitude of prayer and yieldedness.* When I was a college freshman questions about the Bible assignment were mimeographed for us. At the top of the page were the instructions: "Pray for the illumination of the Holy Spirit as you study."

From this class I learned a life-long habit of praying before I study the Bible. Just as I ask God to bless the food before I eat, so I ask God to bless me before I study the Word. I usually pray something like this: "Lord, help me to see things in the Bible I've never seen before and make me understand the difficult passages. Help me to retain as much as possible. Now, I'm completely dependent upon You in this study."

If you have difficulty in Bible study, tell Jesus. If your mind is dull, if you can't concentrate, if you can't remember, if you get sleepy, tell Jesus.

I began pastoring the Westminister Presbyterian Church, Savannah, Georgia, when I was only 19 years old. I was extremely fearful because of my youth. Daily Bible study and prayer, plus a constant sense of the Holy Spirit leading in every decision, got me through many difficult circumstances.

Once an elderly grandmother in the hospital asked me, "How can I have more faith in God?"

I was afraid to admit, "I don't know." So I asked God for an answer. A Scripture verse I had memorized came to mind: "Faith cometh by hearing, and hearing by the word of God" (Romans 10:17).

"You get more faith by learning the Bible," I told her. Then I quoted the verse. I don't know whose need was the greatest at that time, hers or mine; but I'm sure that the answer came from God. On many other occasions God has used the fruit of my Bible study in my life and ministry.

The Bible is like the toolbox in the experienced mechanic's hand. When the old jalopy spits, sputters, and spews, the mechanic unconsciously reaches for the right tools. Because a knowledge of the Bible is useless unless it works in our lives, we should master the Word of God so we can apply its truths without having to search for answers.

STEPS IN BIBLE STUDY

Take Christianity seriously. Set aside a time to *hear, read, study,* and *memorize* the Word of God, and to *meditate* on it. These five words are stepping stones to mastering the Bible.

1. *Hear.* The first step is to listen to the Bible because "Faith cometh by hearing . . ." (Romans 10:17). Listen to the Bible as it is read at church and Sunday School. Give attention to the Word of God as it is taught and preached.

But be careful how you listen to the Bible. Jesus told the parable of the sower, explaining that the different soils represented the different ways men listen to Scripture. Some seeds fell by the wayside and were consumed by birds. This represented people who heard the gospel but allowed Satan to snatch it away before it could take root.

Some seeds fell on stony places without much soil. Because the seed could not put down roots, it withered under the hot sun. This represented people who heard the Bible but did not take the gospel seriously. They wilted under the heat of persecution. Some seeds fell among thorns and germinated but were choked out. This represented people who heard the gospel but let the cares of this world keep them from responding to it.

Finally, some seeds fell on good soil and eventually produced a harvest. This represented people who heard the gospel, believed, and applied it. After this parable, Jesus noted, "Hearing they hear not, neither do they understand" (Matthew 13:13). We should listen sincerely with our heart and with our head.

2. *Read.* Paul counseled Timothy to read the Word: "Till I come, give attendance to reading, to exhortation, to doctrine" (I Timothy 4:13). The great revival under Nehemiah broke out because "they read in the book in

the law of God distinctly, and gave the sense, and caused them to understand the reading" (Nehemiah 8:8). They didn't just read; notice they understood. Let the Son of God illumine your reading. The Bible without the Son is like a sundial lit by the moon.

Read the Bible daily. Don't leave Bible reading up to your inclination; don't wait until you are ready to study the Bible. Some days you won't feel like reading Scripture. You will have to discipline yourself if you are to grow in Bible knowledge. General Douglas McArthur claimed, "Believe me, sir, never a night goes by, be I ever so tired, but I read the Word of God before I go to bed." Develop a daily Bible reading plan. You can read the entire Bible in one year if you read four chapters a day.

A veteran Christian who had long walked with God confessed, "When praying, I am talking to God; when reading the Scripture, He is talking to me. And I'm better off when HE does most of the talking."

Great Christians were once characterized by much prayer, more Bible, and total surrender.

3. *Study.* Paul exhorted Timothy, "Study to shew thyself approved unto God, a workman that needeth not to be ashamed, rightly dividing the word of truth" (II Timothy 2:15). Two facts are seen in this verse. First, you are to study the Bible by giving it your best. Second, you are to divide the Bible, which means slice into it. We personally do our slicing (study) by answering questions.

As a young Christian, you are like those in the first grade. You don't know the material, nor how to study. An effective plan is to begin with a basic Bible study book, one with questions that will make you think your way through each verse. This guide will give you a systematic approach to personal study. Reading will give you breadth; study will give depth.

The first question to ask yourself is, "What does this

passage say?" In other words, you are concerned with the *facts* in the passage. These are often easier to understand in narrative and doctrinal passages than they are in prophetic and poetic passages because they are less likely to be expressed in symbolic terms.

After you have first studied the Bible, it is helpful to have Bible study tools, such as a good reference Bible, an exhaustive concordance, a Bible dictionary, and a Bible commentary or two on hand for unraveling difficult verses. Other valuable helps are a Bible handbook, an atlas, word-study books, and a harmony of the Gospels.

You must remember that the books of the Bible were written long ago and describe concepts and customs which are often foreign to our own culture. Until you understand what God was saying through the various men who wrote the Bible you will have difficulty interpreting its facts. Everything in the Bible should be taken as literally true, except in cases where it is obvious that figurative or symbolic language is being used. Even then, a symbol—simile or metaphor—has a literal interpretation. Never interpret words apart from their literal meaning.

The second question we should ask ourselves about a passage of the Bible is, "What does this passage mean?" In other words, you are concerned about the *principle* underlying the facts. This is not too difficult to determine in narrative passages. There are four types of stories: problem, search, journey, and character change. Each has a climax, a time when the problem is solved, the search is ended, the destination is reached, or the character of a person changes for good or bad. The main principle is usually found at the climax.

For example, the story of the prodigal son, as recorded in Luke 15:11-24, can be reduced to the principle that a loving father forgives a repentant son. Discovering this principle in that passage gives us an eternal truth which we can use today, for our Heavenly Father forgives us when we repent, too.

Finding the main principle in a doctrinal, prophetic, or poetic passage demands that we carefully look for the main idea in that passage. It may have something to do with people, places, times, things, or events. Sometimes there are terms which indicate a summary or conclusion, such as "therefore," "so then," or "wherefore."

It may take considerable time to determine the principle in a passage of Scripture, but if we are patient and depend on the Holy Spirit to reveal it to us, we will find it. A grasp of facts may be primarily a mental thing, but gaining spiritual insights requires something more. Discernment is a special gift from the Lord and it cannot be rushed or forced.

The third question we should ask ourselves about a passage of the Bible is, "What does this passage mean to me?" In other words, you are concerned about the *applications* of the principle of the passage to your life.

There are different ways in which applications are suggested to us. Sometimes you will hear them from pastors, evangelists, teachers and others under whose ministry you sit. Sometimes you will hear them from other students in your classes. Sometimes you hear them in conversations with other believers. Sometimes you discover them in real-life experiences as you go along from day to day. Sometimes you read about them in good Christian books or periodicals. Some applications are simply the voice of the Holy Spirit speaking directly to your heart. Whatever the sources of your applications, they become real only if you use them.

The inductive method of Bible study recognizes that learning moves in stages. The *intellect* analyzes the facts of God's Word as it tries to understand them clearly. The *emotions* respond to the principle drawn out of the facts of a passage and stimulate a person to change. The *will power* takes the principle and applies it to a person's life so that changes are made. The order cannot be reversed for God has made people so they operate in this particular way.

We might compare the process to driving. The automobile represents the Bible. The fuel which gives it power is the Holy Spirit. The owner gets in, turns the key of his yielded will and off he goes.

4. *Memorize.* The next step in Bible study is learning it by heart. The Psalmist declared, "Thy word have I hid in mine heart, that I might not sin against thee" (Psalm 119:11). You will want to memorize portions of Scripture for various reasons. When Jesus was tempted in the wilderness, He quoted Scripture. If you have the Bible in your heart, you too can quote the Scriptures in a moment of trial.

When Philip, a deacon, wanted to witness to the Ethiopian in the chariot he knew Isaiah 53 and used it to lead the eunuch to salvation. Besides using Scripture to combat temptation and as a soul-winning tool, God's Word will guide you into God's will by helping you make difficult decisions.

Memorize Scripture first by underlining the verse in your Bible. Mark the verse so it will stand out the next time you study the passage. Next, write or type the verse on a small card. Carry it with you for review in your free time.

Plan a systematic way to review the verses you have already memorized. Without reviewing, you can't remember the exact words; you may even forget the entire verse. But you will grow in the process of applying diligent effort to master the verse and its meaning.

"Why should I memorize?" a person asked. "The Bible runs through my mind like a sieve."

The Bible is like water. At least it keeps the sieve clean.

The Navigators organization was born during the Second World War when Dawson Trotman challenged servicemen to memorize great numbers of texts. One sailor left his packet of verses lying around and Trotman picked it up to see if the owner could repeat them all.

When he stumbled repeatedly over familiar verses, Trotman said, "That is why the Lord hasn't saved the 240 men on your ship. You do not take the Bible seriously." When you memorize the Bible, you show God you mean business.

5. *Meditate.* The Bible commands us to meditate on its words (Psalm 119:15). This means turning Scripture over and over in your mind. When you wash the dishes, cut the grass, or wait for your wife, meditate on Bible verses you have memorized.

Meditation is going over and over the words in your mind. It's like an old cow in the field, chewing the cud, getting all the goodness he can out of every bite.

The Psalmist indicated that the growing Christian is like the growing tree, prospering because of meditation. "Blessed is the man that walketh not in the counsel of the ungodly, nor standeth in the way of sinners, nor sitteth in the seat of the scornful. But his delight is in the law of the Lord; and in his law doth he meditate . . ." (Psalm 1:1,2). The Psalmist continues, "And he shall be like a tree planted by the rivers of water, that bringeth forth his fruit in his season . . ." (Psalm 1:3).

You should meditate on the Bible because it is a message from God. Because each word has a significance and none is there by error, you should meditate on every word. You can spend a lifetime studying the Bible and never exhaust its depth.

Chapter 5
Make Prayer a Regular Part of Your Life

Recently I met a former high school friend on the streets of Savannah. In school I thought she was pretty, but we had been only casual friends. After reminiscing about old friends she asked, "Why didn't you ever ask me for a date?"

"I didn't think I was good enough." I explained, "You dated the football heroes and fellows with the fancy cars. I didn't think girls cared about me because I was going to be a preacher."

She shook her head in amazement. "I wanted to date you *because* you were going to be a preacher." She told how she had walked by my house hoping I would come out the door. As we talked I remembered the words of Scripture, "Ye have not because ye ask not." I could have dated the girl but didn't ask. Like me, many Christians miss the things God has for them because they don't ask.

Prayer is asking and getting answers from God. Every Christian is invited to go directly to his Father in Heaven: "Ask, and it shall be given you; seek, and ye shall find; knock, and it shall be opened unto you" (Matthew 7:7). Jesus told us, "If ye shall ask any thing in my name, I will do it" (John 14:14). "If ye abide in me . . . ye shall ask what ye will, and it shall be done . . ." (John 15:7). "If we ask any thing according to his will, he heareth us" (I John 5:14). ". . . Ye have not, because ye ask not" (James 4:2).

But prayer is not just asking; it's confession, adoration, thanksgiving and fellowship with God. Some people don't ask for anything, while others ask all the time. They treat God as a Santa Claus. To them prayer is just wishing. We must learn what is the nature of prayer.

THE NATURE OF PRAYER

1. *Prayer is talking with your Heavenly Father.* A father talks to his baby long before the child talks back. Our Heavenly Father did that for us in the Bible. He wrote a message to us long before we were saved. Now we talk back in prayer. God hears our prayers because we are His children.

During the Civil War a little girl tried to get into the White House to see President Lincoln. She wanted a pardon for her father. When she was turned away, she stood crying on the street. Lincoln's son saw her and asked the problem. He took her past the guard where she asked Lincoln to free her dad.

"Any father who raised a little girl like you must be a

good man," Lincoln said in pardoning the father.

When we are Christians, we are related to God through His Son. Jesus takes us past the barriers of Heaven so we can get answers to our requests. To get answers to prayer, sonship is necessary. The New Testament emphasizes this truth, "Now we know that God heareth not sinners: but if any man be a worshipper of God, and doeth his will, him he heareth" (John 9:31). You must become a child of God and know He is your Heavenly Father to get answers to your requests.

If you had a friend but never talked to him or he to you, that would be a strange kind of friendship. So it is with the believer who never talks with God. It is not only men who desire fellowship with God; God desires fellowship with them.

2. *Prayer is the basis of your successful Christian life.* If your next-door neighbor who is a doctor asked you to call him when you got sick but you lived in sickness, it would be your fault. Your neighbor could help you if you asked him, just as God could answer your prayers if you asked Him.

A man traveled to London but had little cash so he skipped breakfast and dinner. The bill included the meals. When he tried to reduce the bill because he didn't eat, the manager said, "It's your fault; the room included meals and the food was on the table."

God wants you to claim "the victory that overcometh the world" (I John 5:4). You do it by prayer. God promises He is "able to do exceeding abundantly above all that we ask or think" (Ephesians 3:20). You get it by prayer; prayer is the doorway to a successful Christian life. Many pray without becoming a triumphant Christian, but no one is triumphant who has not prayed.

Successful Christians experience release from tension when they pray; they find relief from problems. Although prayer is not only a psychological release from anxiety, it certainly does perform that function. Life is wonderful when you cast your cares upon God, realizing He cares for you and will give you grace to endure trials and eventually give you deliverance from them.

Prayer motivates to success. You wait in His presence, which settles you so you can review your life. Your goals become crystal clear. The power needed to successfully reach these goals is bestowed upon the supplicant. Creative answers to your problems are found in prayer, as are new ways to serve the Lord. Prayer shuts out the world. Spiritual discernment is found in the quiet place with God.

Prayer will bring about needed changes in your life. There are some things that will never happen unless you pray. God is sovereign and His will is always done, but it is your responsibility to make petitions known to Him. It is part of His plan that certain things do not take place until men have prayed.

3. *Lack of prayer can be considered sin by the Lord.* If you don't pray, it means you don't trust God or you don't believe God can answer your requests. When our churches don't win souls, it means we haven't prayed. "Therefore to him that knoweth to do good, and doeth it not, to him it is sin" (James 4:17). Believers ought not to be guilty of prayerlessness.

Samuel was very upset when the Israelites demanded he give them a king, but he still promised to pray for them. His sense of responsibility for their spiritual care was so great he said, ". . . God forbid that I should sin against the Lord in ceasing to pray for you: but I will teach you the good and the right way" (I Samuel 12:23). This is evidently one of those "sins of omission" referred to in James 4:17.

THE STEPS OF PRAYER

Prayer is like the cry of a small child in the night. The Psalmist described prayer: "Pour out your heart before him . . ." (Psalm 62:8). You can pray any time, any place, under any condition. But some requests by God's children are more effective than others. Over the long stretch you will want to do more than just cry out. You will want to make your time with God as effective as possible. The following suggestions will help.

1. *Address your prayer to the Father.* Remember, you are praying to God in Heaven. When Jesus was on earth, He followed this formula: He prayed, "Our Father . . ." (Matthew 6:9). Some address their prayers to Jesus or the Holy Spirit. This is not wrong; however, the Bible teaches us to pray to the Father. When Jesus was on earth He reminded His disciples, ". . . in that day ye shall ask me nothing" (John 16:23).

Sometimes people cry at the altar, "Jesus, Jesus, Jesus, Jesus, Jesus . . . ." God understands their heart's desire and answers their cry. But follow God's pattern and you will get God's blessing. Noah followed the blueprint and his ark floated. Moses followed the blueprint in building the tabernacle and God's presence filled the sanctuary. If you follow God's blueprint in prayer, He will answer your requests.

2. *Begin your prayer with adoration.* In the Lord's Prayer, Jesus began by magnifying the Father, ". . . Hallowed be thy name" (Matthew 6:9). As you worship God, you recognize His ability to grant your request.

The Psalms are filled with praise. "Unto thee, O God, do we give thanks, unto thee do we give thanks: for that thy name is near thy wondrous works declare" (Psalm 75:1). Praise is adoration, and God wants His people to magnify Him. "O magnify the Lord with me . . ." (Psalm 34:3). When we use a magnifying glass, the print doesn't get larger; our perception is enlarged. Our praise doesn't change God for He is unchangeable. When we magnify God, our perception is enlarged. We have more faith with which to get answers to our prayers.

3. *Prayer should include thanksgiving.* Paul gave us direction relative to our lives: "In every thing by prayer and supplication with thanksgiving . . ." (Philippians 4:6). When you give thanks you bring salvation into the present tense.

Include in your prayer praise to God for what He has done for you. Thank Him for your salvation . . . for your home . . . for your family . . . for your church . . . for using you. Everyone has something for which to be grateful. When you recognize what God has done in the past, you have a basis for expecting future answers to prayer.

4. *You must confess your sin.* Since we are always sinners (I John 1:8), we must always ask God to forgive us of our sins. Include in your prayer confession of your sins to God and a request for forgiveness. You can't be in an offensive position with a person and get him to give you something. David said, "I acknowledged my sin unto thee, and mine iniquity have I not hid. I said, I will confess my transgressions unto the Lord; and thou forgavest the iniquity of my sin . . ." (Psalm 32:5). The best-known Biblical prayer of confession is probably that found in Psalm 51. Read it the next time your sin keeps you from praying.

If you owe your doctor a bill which you won't pay, be careful about getting sick. He might not treat you. Or, you might be embarrassed and have to apologize, "I'm sorry I haven't paid you. I will pay you, but please help my son." Likewise, you may have to tell God, "I'm sorry for my sin; please help me." Live clean; you never know when you may desperately need to pray.

To the believer in fellowship with God, He says, "Call unto me, and I will answer thee, and shew thee great and mighty things, which thou knowest not" (Jeremiah 33:3).

Jesus suggested the model for intercession: "And forgive us our debts, as we forgive our debtors" (Matthew 6:12). We must clean up our life before we can pray. We must confess every time we pray because we are sinners even after we pray. The Bible teaches, "If we say that we have no sin, we deceive ourselves . . ." (I John 1:8).

5. *Make reconciliation with others.* Since prayer is talking with a Holy God, you must forgive others as you ask God to cleanse you. Jesus said, "For if ye forgive men their trespasses, your heavenly Father will also forgive you" (Matthew 6:14-15). This may require reconciliation with someone who has offended you in some way (Matthew 5:23-24).

6. *Pray for your personal needs.* Jesus taught us to pray, "Give us this day our daily bread" (Matthew 6:11). Paul said, "Be careful for nothing; but in every thing by prayer and supplication with thanksgiving let your requests be made known unto God. And the peace of God, which passeth all understanding, shall keep your hearts and minds through Christ Jesus" (Philippians 4:6-7). This is the privilege extended to believers, and they ought to take advantage of it every day.

Curtis Hutson delivered mail for his livelihood and also pastored the Forrest Hills Baptist Church in Decatur, Georgia. By faith he resigned the post office position; he was receiving only $75 a month from the church. His house payments alone were $92 a month.

In a couple of months, the bills mounted, so he made a pile on the kitchen table. At 2:00 a.m. he and his wife, on their knees, prayed, "God, if I have to go back to the post office, You'll be embarrassed."

A couple awoke, talked about their pastor, got out of bed, and brought a check to his house in the middle of the night. It was for the exact amount of the bills on the table.

7. *Prayer should include intercession for the needs of others.* Paul said, "Brethren, my heart's desire and prayer to God for Israel is, that they might be saved" (Romans 10:1). Paul usually reminded those to whom he wrote that he was praying for them (Romans 1:9; Philippians 1:4; Colossians 1:3; I Thessalonians 1:2).

Only a selfish person would pray constantly for himself. It is unlikely God would honor the request a person makes only for his own needs.

8. *Conclude your prayers in Jesus' name.* You should conclude your prayers in the name of Jesus. He instructed us, "If ye shall ask any thing in my name, I will do it" (John 14:14).

How can sinners come into the presence of a Holy God? We cannot come in ourselves; we must stand dressed in the righteousness of Jesus Christ, ". . . that we might be made the righteousness of God in him." (II Corinthians 5:21). When we stand before God the Father in His Son, we have all the perfection and purity of Jesus Christ. This is because of His shed blood on Calvary. We add Christ's name at the end of the prayer because in using the proper conclusion we recognize we are in Him and He is our Advocate who "ever liveth to make intercession" for us (Hebrews 7:25).

We should not feel obligated to include all of these things in every prayer we offer up to God, for there are times when we just express one thought. However, the eight elements described above are important to structured prayers, such as those we hear in a public worship service or pray in our own private devotions.

THE BASIS OF ANSWERED PRAYER

"But I ask and my prayers are never answered," you might say. Maybe there is something choking them. Perhaps a sin pointed out here will flash in your mind. If so, do something about it so you can receive answers to your prayers.

1. *Your prayers are answered when you obey God.* God is our Heavenly Father and He loves His children. We can go to Him just like a child who asks things of his earthly father.

A little boy often went to see his dad at the hardware store and each time asked for a nickel to buy a cold drink from the machine in the supply-room. When Dad was angry, he didn't get the nickel. The little boy was careful to stay on Dad's good side when he wanted a cold drink.

"And whatsoever we ask, we receive of him, because we keep his commandments, and do those things that are pleasing in his sight" (I John 3:22). Note that we get *whatsoever* when we keep His commandments and please God.

A teenage son asked to borrow his father's car for a date. He felt the family car was more luxurious than his.

"No!" was the answer. "The other day I asked you to wash it and sweep out the sand, but you didn't have time." Within 30 minutes the boy was back to tell his father the car was clean and to again ask to borrow it.

The Christian who disobeys God doesn't have the freedom to pray to his Heavenly Father and get the answers he seeks, without first seeking forgiveness.

The Bible tells us the prayers of the righteous are effective. We are never righteous by our own efforts; our righteousness is imputed by Jesus Christ. However, there is a sense in which we are righteous. This means "doing right." If we want our prayers answered, we must do right by paying our bills, not cursing, going to church, tithing, witnessing, and doing all the other things we know are right.

"Confess your faults one to another, and pray one for another, that ye may be healed. The effectual fervent prayer of a righteous man availeth much" (James 5:16). The phrase *availeth much* means "makes tremendous things available." When you are right with God, your prayers make the greatest things in the world available.

2. *Your prayers are answered when you get rid of known sin.* The Bible teaches that our sin makes it impossible for God to hear us. "If I regard iniquity in my heart, the Lord will not hear me" (Psalm 66:18). Iniquity is sin, doing the exact opposite of God's will. If God tells us not to take His name in vain and we do, how can we ask Him to answer our prayers?

There is another verse that says we plug up God's ears. "Behold, the Lord's hand is not shortened, that it cannot save; neither his ear heavy, that it cannot hear: but your iniquities have separated between you and your God, and your sins have hid his face from you, that he will not hear" (Isaiah 59:1-2). God has the ability to help us and His ears can hear us, but our sin makes it impossible.

Robert was a mischievous boy. When his mother was angry he hid in his favorite hiding place, a dark closet, where she couldn't see or hear him. When Robert was hiding was not the time to ask his mother for money to go to the store for ice cream. If you have sin in your life, get rid of it; then ask God for your petition. Only then can you get answers to prayer.

3. *Your prayers are answered when you abide in Christ.* Jesus promised, "If ye abide in me, and my words abide in you, ye shall ask what ye will, and it shall be done unto you" (John 15:7). The word *abide* means to join yourself to God without any obstruction. It does not mean to hang on to God. When a branch is just hanging

on to the vine, it usually withers. But when the branch is growing from the vine, it prospers and has fruit.

Just as the branch allows the life-giving sap to flow through it, the Christian who abides in Christ and His Word as a part of his life, allows the Holy Spirit to control him.

We allow important people to do most of the talking and we ask them only pertinent questions. Likewise, when we allow God to speak to our heart through the Bible, we are prepared to ask the right request.

4. *Your prayers are answered when you ask according to His will.* God has a will which is His desire for us. It is God's will that we pray for the things He wants us to have.

I always looked forward to a visit from my Uncle Herman who usually brought candy. But I had to ask for it. Sometimes I had to rummage through his pockets to find the candy. It gave Uncle Herman as much happiness to give me the candy as it did for me to find it. "And this is the confidence that we have in him, that, if we ask any thing according to his will, he heareth us: and if we know that he hear us, whatsoever we ask, we know that we have the petitions that we desired of him" (I John 5:14-15).

We must pray according to God's will. Once I prayed outside of God's will. While going through Bible college, I prayed for money. There was a hole-in-one contest at a nearby golf course. Every person who hit the ball in the cup got $200. I prayed that God would help me make a hole-in-one. I knelt on the golf tee and asked God to guide my swing. None of the balls went into the cup.

This was not God's way of providing for my financial needs. There was an element of gambling in the contest. Also, I used to enjoy playing golf and wanted some glory for getting a hole-in-one.

How can you know if the things you ask are His will?

Certain things are obviously God's will, such as people being saved. God wants everyone to be saved (II Peter 3:9). It is not God's nature to frustrate His children; however, we may have to go through several doors, or stages of prayer to arrive at an answer to prayer. God tests our sincerity. We need to go through each open door as it appears. It may take a while to get an answer to prayer, but we should pray with confidence. Our Heavenly Father doesn't play games with us, hiding His will like Easter eggs, hoping we will find it.

5. *Your prayers are answered when you ask in faith.* Faith is expecting an answer. As a schoolboy I sent coupons off for magic rings, code books and other trinkets. Every day I'd ask the mailman, "Did it come today?"

"Not today," the postman would say. "Maybe tomorrow." I'd get so excited I could hardly wait for the postman to come.

When we pray we have to believe that the answer is coming. "Therefore I say unto you, What things soever ye desire, when ye pray, believe that ye receive them, and ye shall have them" (Mark 11:24). The sincerity of our faith determines the answers we get. "He that cometh to God must believe that he is, and that he is a rewarder of them that diligently seek him" (Hebrews 11:6).

When I was a child I asked my mother for a quarter to go downtown. Twenty-five cents paid for the streetcar, popcorn, and a cold drink. I never asked for a dollar because I knew she wouldn't give it. I asked for what I felt she would give me—twenty-five cents. "But let him ask in faith, nothing wavering. For he that wavereth is like a wave of the sea driven with the wind and tossed" (James 1:6).

It's obvious some of us need more faith, not more time in prayer. Therefore we ask, *How do we get more faith?*

One way is to pray for it. Faith is sending off the coupon, then going to the mailbox every day looking for the answer. Expect answers from God. Build yourself a spiritual mailbox. "I got a reply this morning," you can tell your friends.

6. *Your prayers are answered when your motives are right.* When we come to God in prayer, our desires must be pure. The Bible tells us that we sometimes do not get answers because of our lusts (selfish desires). "Ye ask, and receive not, because ye ask amiss, that ye may consume it upon your lusts" (James 4:3).

After salvation, I immediately began praying for a car. I had been poor all my life. "Dear God, give me a car," I prayed sincerely, then added, "If you give me a car, I'll pick up people and take them to church." I was bargaining with God. However, God looked through the words and saw my selfish desire. I wanted a car to take girls on dates and to impress the boys. God didn't answer the request.

Years later, I became a pastor and still didn't have a car. I made my pastoral calls on a bicycle. In God's time, the members of the church got together and bought me a car. When your motives are right and you are willing to do anything to accomplish God's will, God will give you a car or whatever you need—in His own time.

7. *Your prayers are answered when you live peaceably with your mate.* Some husbands and wives fight. The Bible commands that husband and wife live together peacefully so that their prayers can be answered. "Likewise, ye husbands, dwell with them according to knowledge, giving honour unto the wife, as unto the weaker vessel, and as being heirs together of the grace of life; that your prayers be not hindered" (I Peter 3:7). When a husband argues constantly with his wife, how can the children see Christ in their father? Then, if the father and mother

pray for their child to be saved, their arguments have made it impossible for their prayer to be heard.

PRACTICAL HELPS FOR PRAYER

Giving practical helps for prayer is similar to telling a child how to ask his father for things. However, some children don't get their requests because they ask in the wrong way.

1. *Make a prayer list.* This is an itemized list of things you want from God. Some people place the items on one side of a sheet of paper; the other side is left blank to record the answers.

A prayer list gives you discipline in praying. A prayer list will challenge you to keep praying until you finish your obligations. A prayer list adds incentive to your faith. You'll be encouraged when you look over the answers to your prayers. It will provoke you to greater prayer.

2. *Find a private place.* A regular place for private prayer is necessary. Jesus was disgusted with the hypocritical ways of the religious leaders of His day, those who loved to pray on street corners and in synagogues to receive the praise of men. Therefore, He taught His followers to find a private "closet" where they could be alone with the Lord (Matthew 6:5-6).

It is not always easy to find a secluded spot for prayer, but we can generally work it out. There is something about associating a particular activity with a particular place which is helpful, although we know we can pray anywhere.

Perhaps your "closet" would be your bedroom or the den when the kids have gone to school. Some businessmen pray in their private offices. You must find the place that is the best for you. However, you can pray in the crowded waiting room of an airline terminal. You can pray with your eyes open as you drive on the expressway. But a quiet place is better. You won't be distracted or embarrassed. Two lovers will talk anywhere just to be together, but they would rather talk in private.

3. *Make a regular schedule.* Try to schedule the same time each day for prayer. If you wait until you have time, it will never happen. You must make time to commune with God. Then, don't pray because you are required to do it, but pray because you need it and desire it. Prayer is more than a few seconds' grace before the meal. Since prayer gives us our greatest victory and is our greatest strength, we should give it our serious consideration and the best time of the day.

Jesus said men "ought always to pray . . ." (Luke 18:1), and Paul said to "pray without ceasing" (I Thessalonians 5:17), suggesting that prayer at any time is appropriate. This is true, of course, but there is something about associating a particular time with prayer which is helpful in maintaining the habit.

4. *The posture of prayer.* Some believers are convinced they must kneel to pray, thus showing humility and contrition before God. They take their example from Paul who said, "I bow my knees unto the Father of our Lord Jesus Christ" (Ephesians 3:14). However, in the Bible we can find examples of people who prayed while standing (Jeremiah 18:20), sitting (II Samuel 7:18), or lying prostrate (Matthew 26:39), while some prayed with their hands lifted upward (I Kings 8:22; Psalm 28:2; I Timothy 2:8).

The important thing is not the position of the body, but the condition of the heart. Christians today usually bow their heads to show reverence and close their eyes to shut out distractions while praying, but we ought not to become legalistic about these things.

5. *Study Bible prayers.* You will get your greatest

answers to prayer when you pray like the men of Scripture. When Moses prayed, Israel prevailed in battle. When Daniel prayed, the lions' mouths were stopped. When Elijah prayed, it didn't rain for three and a half years. When you follow the successful ingredients of the prayers of godly men, you are more likely to have success than if you create your own prayer patterns.

After you get up off your knees, put your prayers to work. The old saint reminded, "The best place to pray for potatoes is at the end of a potato hoe."

PART III

Fellowshipping With a Church

Chapter 6
Your First Public Act Is Baptism

I was meeting people as they came down the aisle at Thomas Road Baptist Church when a young man came forward to yield himself to teach Sunday School.

"You're a member of this church," I said with a positive voice as I filled out the card used at the altar.

"No, I don't believe in baptism," he told me in a matter-of-fact voice.

"You can't teach Sunday School here if you're not baptized," was my reply.

WHO SHOULD BE BAPTIZED

Baptism is the new believer's first step of faith. He announces to the world that he has placed his faith in the Lord Jesus Christ and his life from now on is going to be lived for Him.

The man mentioned above and I discussed the subject of baptism at length and I gave him these reasons for the necessity of baptism.

1. *You should be baptized because it is the first step of obedience.* Every Christian should be baptized immediately after he is saved because baptism is not optional; it is commanded after salvation.

There is no record in the New Testament of an unbaptized believer who, given the chance, refused to follow God's plan. The repentant thief on the cross entered Paradise upon his death without baptism, but he was not given the opportunity. From his cry, we can determine that he was willing to do anything to receive eternal life. Death wounds were eating away his life; baptism could not have saved him. The death of Christ was mandatory for the thief on the cross. Its symbol, baptism, is just as mandatory so the Christian can testify to the world of his identification with Christ.

Jesus commanded, "Go ye into all the world, and preach the gospel to every creature. He that believeth and is baptized shall be saved; but he that believeth not shall be damned" (Mark 16:15-16). The verse should not be interpreted as meaning baptism saves; of course it does not. The main point is that Jesus tied baptism to belief. Baptism is tied to belief in Matthew's account also, "Go ye therefore, and teach all nations, baptizing them in the name of the Father, and of the Son, and of the Holy Ghost" (Matthew 28:19).

John the Baptist identified baptism as a sign of the forgiveness of sin. "I indeed baptize you with water unto repentance: but he that cometh after me is mightier than I, whose shoes I am not worthy to bear: he shall baptize you with the Holy Ghost, and with fire" (Matthew 3:11). The baptism of John had a different symbol than baptism today. Those who submitted to John's baptism were turning from their sins and looking forward for the coming Messiah. Today, baptism looks *back* at Christ's death, burial and resurrection. By being submerged in water, the followers of John the Baptist took the first step of obedience to the message of God.

On the Day of Pentecost, Peter tied baptism to conversion. He cried out, "Repent, and be baptized every one of you in the name of Jesus Christ for the remission of sins, and ye shall receive the gift of the Holy Ghost" (Acts 2:38). Those who believed the gospel had to demonstrate it by the public act of baptism. Baptism did not save because the Scriptures bear out, "Then they that gladly received his word were baptized" (Acts 2:41).

Receiving the Word of God was the *cause* that brought salvation; baptism was the *result*. That day, 3,000 received the Word of God and were baptized. They did so immediately. A church should keep its baptistry filled and ready for use because someone may walk forward during the morning service and receive the Word of God. They should be allowed to immediately take the first step of obedience, the result of salvation, which is baptism.

2. *You should be baptized because of the example of Christ.* The ordeal of God becoming flesh is called the humiliation (Philippines 2:8). Even though Jesus was King, He did not demand royal treatment. Christ came as a servant (Philippians 2:7). John was baptizing in the River of Jordan for the repentance of sin. Jesus could not repent from sin for He knew no sin. Five times in the New Testament we are told that the Son of God was sinless (John 18:38; II Corinthians 5:21; Hebrews 4:15; I Peter 2:22; I John 3:5). If ever there was a person who didn't need to be baptized, it was Jesus Christ. Even John the Baptist realized this for he said, "I have need to be baptized of thee, and comest thou to me?" (Matthew 3:14).

Yet Jesus *was* baptized because in God's plan it was necessary. First, He was baptized to identify with the remnant of Israel. These were the ones He came to save. Second, He was baptized to fulfill all righteousness. "And Jesus answering said unto him, Suffer it to be so now: for thus it becometh us to fulfil all righteousness. Then he suffered him" (Matthew 3:15). Here Jesus was revealing Himself as the predicted Messiah in the Old Testament, the One coming to bring righteousness to His people.

Jesus was baptized to publicly announce the beginning of His ministry. Up until this time, He had not preached or performed miracles. His baptism launched His ministry. In parallel manner, the Levitical priest was immersed in water at age 30 as a public sign of the beginning of His ministry. Jesus, a Priest after the order of Melchizedek, fulfilled the sign by being baptized at age 30.

John was called the Baptizer and Jesus came to him; the order was not reversed. Since Jesus obeyed God's plan of baptism, we should follow His example and be baptized accordingly. If you have not followed God's plan for baptism, you should seek out a person who can baptize you.

Some ladies think it is unsophisticated to appear soaking wet before the congregation, their pretty hairdo washed out. Remember, Jesus Christ submitted to the same ordinance before the crowds of soldiers, slaves, Pharisees and businessmen. But more, the angels of Heaven must have witnessed Jesus Christ submitting to baptism. Jesus was baptized and later He would ask others to follow His example.

Even after Christ had died, been buried, was resurrected, and had ascended to Heaven, there were those who were limited to preaching about John's baptism unto repentance, rather than preaching the New Testament meaning of baptism (Acts 18:25; 19:3). In such cases, Christians explained what was lacking and the people involved were then re-baptized in the name of Christ.

3. *You should be baptized because of the example of the early Christians.* Soul-winners in the New Testament believed in baptism; everyone who accepted Christ was baptized: 3,000 on the Day of Pentecost, Paul, Cornelius and his household, the Ethiopian eunuch, new believers in Samaria, Lydia, the Philippian jailor, and many others. Their example should motivate every young Christian to be baptized. Since every new convert in the New Testament who could be baptized was baptized, why should any put it off today?

It has been a long time since this author has heard a sermon on baptism. But this has not always been the case. Once, Baptist churches preached often on baptism. Great debates were held on it. Church members were constantly reminded of what they believed concerning baptism. However, today most churches just baptize after they preach the gospel.

This is God's pattern. There are no great sermons on baptism in the New Testament; they just baptized. Neither are there long doctrinal dissertations or a lot of commands to be baptized. Jesus commanded baptism and the early church practiced it. In the book of Romans, Paul explained baptism (6:3-6) because the nature of the book is a systematic coverage of salvation. Baptism had to be included in the overall plan of God for the Christian.

4. *You should be baptized to tell the world that you are a Christian.* Is there such a thing as a secret believer? Yes. All a man has to do to become saved is believe and receive Christ. After reading the Word of God, a man can believe in Jesus Christ and become a child of God. He

does not have to be baptized for salvation. He does not have to confess publicly in order to be saved. Therefore, he can be a secret believer—but he shouldn't be.

If a man is obedient, he will be baptized. The new Christian will place himself before the church. When he is buried in the water, he tells the world that he has died with Christ. Under the water, he is identified with the burial of Christ. When he is brought up, it symbolizes his resurrection with Christ. The new Christian is telling the world that he now has the life of Christ (Romans 6:4-6).

In Moslem country when a man believes in Jesus Christ he is usually ignored. But when he is baptized, this is a public repudiation of Islam. Baptism is a public embrace of Jesus Christ. Because of this, many new Christians are thrown out of their families, ostracized from the community, and even persecuted to death.

Apparently this is what happened in the New Testament; some were killed because of their baptism, "Else what shall they do which are baptized for the dead, if the dead rise not at all? why are they then baptized for the dead?" (I Corinthians 15:29). Paul is discussing the subject of resurrection in this passage and was saying here that new converts being baptized and taking the place of believers who had died, did so because they were convinced that the Christian life was worthwhile and some day they would rise from the dead and inherit eternal life. No one can be baptized by proxy, for the only valid kind is that involving the believer himself.

Some churches have maintained that a new Christian ought to "prove himself" before he submits to baptism. These churches conduct communicant classes to prepare the believers for baptism. The thought is to protect the church's purity against those who are baptized too early and later drop out of attendance, embarrassing the local congregation.

On the other side of the coin, however, the public confession of baptism may strengthen a new believer. He publicly announces to the world that he is going to follow Jesus Christ. Now the unsaved community expects him to live like a Christian, and the Christian community will encourage him. God has strengthened many young Christians because they have honestly obeyed God through baptism. Many have won spiritual battles sooner than they could have otherwise because they took this first obedient stand for Christ.

5. *You should be baptized because it fulfills a symbol of salvation.* The heart and core of salvation is the death of Jesus Christ. His death was more than an example of humanitarian sympathy. Christ died as a substitute for sinners (Matthew 20:28). When He died, He took your punishment. Christ took your place. God placed you in His Son on Calvary. Because of this, Paul testified, "I am crucified with Christ: nevertheless I live . . ." (Galatians 2:20).

But this substitution goes a step further. You were buried with Him and when you came up out of the grave with Christ, you were given a new life (Romans 6:4-6). Therefore, you ought to be baptized to fulfill the symbol of Christ's death on Calvary.

The author began his Christian life as a Presbyterian and was licensed by the Savannah, Georgia Presbytery, but later became a Baptist minister. The argument that convinced me to submit to immersion was spiritual baptism: since I was placed into His death, burial, and resurrection, I ought to fulfill the symbol and be placed into water as He commanded.

Christian baptism denotes identification with a local church through being placed into the body of Christ which this represents. The church is not simply an organization established by men. It is an organism created by God Himself, and the Lord Jesus Christ dwells in the midst of His people (Matthew 16:18; 18:20). Believers become members of Christ's body when they receive Christ. "But now hath God set the members every one of them in the body, as it hath pleased him . . . Now ye are the body of Christ, and members in particular" (I Corinthians 12:18,27).

Paul wrote that God "hath put all things under his [Christ's] feet, and gave him to be the head over all things to the church, which is his body, the fulness of him that filleth all in all" (Ephesians 1:22-23). Other parallel passages include Ephesians 4:15,16 and Colossians 2:18,19. The church is also referred to as a building and a holy temple in Ephesians 2:19-22 and I Peter 2:5.

6. *You should be baptized to have a good conscience before God.* You cannot do anything to gain merit before God. Salvation is by grace through faith. All you can do is receive the free gift of eternal life. We are told salvation is "not of works, lest any man should boast" (Ephesians 2:9), and "not by works of righteousness which we have done" (Titus 3:5). Baptism cannot add to your salvation, nor can baptism secure your salvation so you can't lose it. Baptism cannot even illuminate your salvation so you can understand it, nor magnify your salvation so you can better serve Him. Baptism is simply obedience to Jesus Christ. The hymn writer concludes, "Trust and obey for there's no other way to be happy in Jesus."

When you have been baptized you fulfill the Scripture, "The like figure whereunto even baptism doth also now save us (not the putting away of the filth of the flesh, but the answer of a good conscience toward God)" (I Peter 3:21). When you have been baptized, you know you have done all that God has required. Your conscience is at peace. Therefore, you ought to be happy and confident in your Christian life.

WHO SHOULD NOT BE BAPTIZED

When Christ gave His Great Commission to followers on a mountain in Galilee, He made it very clear that they were to first make disciples and then to baptize them "in the name of the Father, and of the Son, and of the Holy Ghost." Then His disciples were commanded, "teaching them to observe all things whatsoever I have commanded" (Matthew 28:19,20).

On the Day of Pentecost, Peter made it very clear that baptism followed conversion. He said, "Repent, and be baptized every one of you in the name of Jesus Christ for the remission of sins, and ye shall receive the gift of the Holy Ghost . . . Then they that gladly received his word were baptized: and the same day there were added unto them about three thousand souls" (Acts 2:38,41).

1. *Anyone who does not believe on Christ should not be baptized.* Infants and others not accountable mentally should not be baptized until they are able to become believers. There is no "saving power" in baptism.

The church went along for several centuries before the practice of infant baptism came into vogue. It has been used widely in all branches of what might be loosely called "Christendom." Some think of it as only a dedication on the part of pious parents who hope to guide their children to a salvation experience later in life, but unfortunately many think of it as a saving ordinance for their children.

Many problems stem from this viewpoint; the worst is the fact that individuals, baptized as infants, grow up thinking they are saved and, therefore, see no need to repent and seek forgiveness for their sins. They are doomed to eternal condemnation just as much as those who were never baptized as infants.

2. *Innocent children and people not accountable mentally are provided for by a gracious God.* The question is

raised as to what happens to children who die before they reach an age of accountability to God and, therefore, have not had a salvation experience. King David was convinced that his dead infant son went to the place of the righteous dead, for he said, ". . . I shall go to him, but he shall not return to me" (II Samuel 12:23). He was sure the child was in the presence of God.

The word *safe,* not *saved,* is used of such children. They are safe in God, although not saved in the normal meaning of that word. Jesus said, "Suffer the little children to come unto me, and forbid them not; for of such is the kingdom of God" (Mark 10:14). He seemed to imply by this that innocent children and those limited in intelligence by mental retardation will enter Heaven.

The Bible teaches, we believe, what is called "believer's baptism." Only individuals who have believed on Christ as their personal Saviour are eligible to participate in this.

Of the six reasons why you should be baptized, any one of the points should tell a person he needs to be baptized. The force of all six leaves a believer who refuses baptism in disobedience, but no one should be argued into baptism. The very hint that some Christians in the New Testament were baptized should motivate every Christian to seek it. Today's believers should not want to live less than those who were closest to the Lord.

A Presbyterian lady once confessed: "I'd like to be immersed, but I just hate to give in to the Baptists." Her willingness to be baptized was correct; her motives were wrong. She should have realized immersion is "giving in" to Christ. He set the example in immersion and later gave the command regarding baptism.

Chapter 7
Why You Should Be Related To A Church

My brother Richard had not been baptized. He was saved but didn't want to join a Baptist church. My arguments on baptism by immersion never fully convinced him until he heard me preach a sermon on "Why a church should be growing." I pointed out that growing churches are obeying the Scriptures and people are being baptized.

He came forward and was baptized, explaining, "My former church wasn't getting people saved so it must not be right." The presence of God bringing people to Christ in a growing church convinced him to be baptized.

A lady came forward after I preached in a church in

Kansas City, telling me she wanted rededication. I asked if her membership was in that church.

"No," she whispered, "I promised mama I would stay in her church." I explained to her that the book of Acts gives illustrations of people taking a letter of introduction from their home church to their new residence.

Then I asked, "Did it ever occur to you that you may have backslidden because your membership was not in a church that could watch over you?"

WHY YOU SHOULD JOIN A CHURCH

We are fast moving into the "un-church" age of Christianity. Some think they can stay home on Sunday morning and watch church on television and they have fulfilled their obligations to God. Others attend a home Bible class, while many do not go to church at all, but claim to be Christians. It is difficult to see how a Christian can be spiritual without belonging to a local church.

In recent years we have heard arguments against being connected to an organized church. Cell groups meeting in people's homes become substitutes for regular churches. As good as Christian television programs, cell groups, and other organizations might be, none can take the place of a church.

How can an adequate program of instruction for various age groups be provided without a church? How can worship be given a prominent place in a community without a church? How can an expanded sense of fellowship among believers be promoted without a church? How can effective Christian service projects be coordinated without a church?

It is difficult to maintain your spirituality without the support and fellowship of a local body of believers. Many, such as those in nursing homes or those in prisons, are growing spiritually without the benefit of organized services, of course, but it makes the road between here and Heaven mighty lonely.

1. *Church membership fulfills the symbol of baptism.* Every person is a sinner and deserves death. But Christ died on Calvary to take the place of every sinner. He died that the sinner might not die, but have eternal life. When Christ hung on Calvary, God took the believing sinner and placed him into Jesus Christ. Technically this is called the vicarious, substitutionary atonement. In fact, it means that when Christ died, the sinner died. Paul witnessed this identification: "I am crucified with Christ: nevertheless I live; yet not I, but Christ liveth in me . . ." (Galatians 2:20).

To become a Christian, all the sinner has to do is believe on Jesus Christ (Acts 16:31). After salvation, the first step of obedience is baptism. When the new Christian is placed under the water, he testifies to the world that he has died with Christ. Coming out of the water is a picture of his resurrection with Christ.

The symbol of being placed into Christ is fulfilled when the person is placed in the water. "Know ye not, that so many of us as were baptized into Jesus Christ were baptized into his death? Therefore we are buried with him by baptism into death: that like as Christ was raised up from the dead by the glory of the Father, even so we also should walk in newness of life" (Romans 6:3,4).

When you are baptized, you become a member of a local church. The Bible describes the church as the body of Christ—". . . the church, which is his body . . ." (Ephesians 1:22-23). Just as you were actually placed into Christ on Calvary for salvation, you fulfill the symbol by being placed into His local body, the church. This is done by baptism.

The symbol is important to God. Many of God's children in the Old Testament violated His symbols and were punished. When Samson cut his hair he told the world he no longer obeyed God. His strength was not in his hair; it was only a symbol that his strength was in God. The children of Israel were to look to the brazen serpent on the pole if they wanted to live (John 3:14); those who refused the symbol died. These symbols had no power in themselves but reflected obedience to God.

Since baptism is a symbol of being placed into Christ's body, we destroy His symbol when we are not baptized. Also, we disobey His command (Matthew 28:19). We are baptized initially into Christ; now we can reflect that baptism by weekly placing ourselves with other believers in His local body. We do this by attending church.

2. *Church membership places you under the ministry of the Word of God.* Every Christian should be in the Lord's house every week so he can learn the Word of God. One of the primary purposes of the church is to teach the Scriptures. Immediately upon the first manifestation of the church after the Day of Pentecost, the people put themselves under doctrine (Acts 2:42). The early church taught more often than Sunday: "And daily in the temple, and in every house, they ceased not to *teach* and preach Jesus Christ" (Acts 5:42; emphasis mine). You ought to be in church so you can be under the ministry of the Word of God.

Knowledge of the Bible will cause you: to grow (I Peter 2:2); to abstain from sin (Psalm 119:105); to have your prayers answered (John 15:5); to be like Christ (I Corinthians 3:23); and to strengthen your faith (Romans 10:13). Those who don't study the Bible backslide and sometimes corrupt those about them. Since it is mandatory to study the Word of God and the church is God's instrument for teaching it, a Christian ought to be a faithfully attending member of a church.

3. *Church membership helps you grow through fellow-*

ship. God's Word commands that we not forsake "the assembling of ourselves together . . ." (Hebrews 10:25). It was not mere chance that God chose the word *together* in this verse. When Christians come together, there is a mutual interaction, a give-and-take relationship. This does not mean that Christians give up their doctrine or convictions. Fellowship is not necessarily consensus, which is like water seeking its lowest level. Rather, when Christians give-and-take, they give to one another and take something back in return. This is fellowship. Christians grow through fellowship.

Some churches announce, "There will be a fellowship after the evening service," where Christians drink coffee and chat. This activity is very enjoyable, but Biblical fellowship is much deeper than making small talk and having refreshments.

Fellowship involves revealing yourself to other people as you really are. First you confess that you are a sinner; second, you confess your need of reliance upon God to work out all things in your life; third, you confess that you cannot live for God by yourself; and fourth, you confess a need for the way of life found in the local church. You become like those with whom you fellowship.

Concerning fellowship, John wrote, "If we walk in the light, as he is in the light, we have fellowship one with another, and the blood of Jesus Christ his Son cleanseth us from all sin" (I John 1:7). This verse teaches that as a Christian you should attempt to do the very best you can to keep the commandments of God. This is walking in the light, whereby you follow the example of Jesus Christ who is the Light of the world (John 8:12).

When you walk in the light, you have fellowship with other children of God. If they are conscientiously serving Jesus Christ, they also will be a church where fellowship is experienced. A conscious endeavor to serve Christ means that as a Christian you will submit yourself to God and to one another. Yieldedness to God is the basis of fellowship with one another. The blood of Jesus Christ covers those who are fellowshipping together. Fellowship is not the basis for forgiving sin, but you who experience fellowship have followed the New Testament requirements by confessing your sins (I John 1:9); hence, the blood has cleansed you and you are forgiven.

It has been said, "You can't be a Christian alone," meaning a person cannot grow in his Christian life without getting along with other people. God is not looking for the hermit to "come apart from the world" by climbing a pole. God is looking for believers to work out their faith in relationship to others.

4. *Church membership is taught by the example of the early church.* Those who attempt to live for Christ outside the local church deny the example set for them in Scripture. As you examine the pages of the New Testament you find Christians joining with other Christians to hear the Word of God (Acts 2:42; 5:42; 19:9-10). They also fellowshipped together (Acts 2:42), and they joined their hearts together in prayer (Acts 4:24). The local church was a launching pad for evangelism; they went out together to win lost people to Jesus Christ (Acts 5:42; 20:20,31). You will not find occasions of Christians going it alone. Wherever Paul went he organized Christians into churches (Acts 15:41).

Before they were saved the Jews brought their money to the temple. The early Christians brought their money to the church. They laid it at the apostles' feet (Acts 4:34,35). The apostles used this money to provide for widows (Acts 6:1). They also gave to needy saints (Acts 11:29,30), and to carry out the work of evangelism (Philippians 4:18). The early Christians were loyal in their financial giving to the church. Some gave all that they had (Acts 2:45), while others gave according to their ability (Acts 11:29).

5. *Church membership is taught by the principles of "God's place" for worship in the Old Testament.* God has always had a place for corporate worship, even though there are illustrations of man individually worshiping God in various places and circumstances. First, the tabernacle was God's place for centralized worship, and He cautioned His people that they should not worship at other than the designated place (Deuteronomy 12:2-4,11).

Later, God's place for worship was the temple in Jerusalem. Whenever man got away from God's place, he began worshiping as he pleased. The principle of "God's place" does not tie salvation to sacrificing the blood of animals in the Old Testament. It became a man-made religion when individuals began worshiping God at a place that was contrary to God's commandment.

Just as God required His people to assemble for corporate worship in a certain spot in the Old Testament, so He has a place for corporate worship in the New Testament. This is the church. This does not, of course, exclude individual worship, for in both Testaments man has access to God at any time and any place.

The three characteristics of God's corporate place of worship are seen in Deuteronomy 12:1-32. First, God required His people to assemble for worship where He promised to meet with them (Deuteronomy 12:1). God's presence in the tabernacle and later in the temple was an invitation for His people to assemble. Second, God's place was located where the symbols of redemption were celebrated. In the Old Testament, these symbols were the blood sacrifice and the furniture of the tabernacle. Third, the people were commanded to assemble for worship where they would find God's man (Deuteronomy 12:19).

In the New Testament, the local church meets the three requirements mentioned above for God's place. First, the church has God's presence. Remember, a church is not a building but an assembly of people. God has promised to be with them when they are assembled together (Matthew 18:20; Acts 4:31; Hebrews 10:25). The church is called a candlestick (Revelation 1:20; 2:1,5), and the candle is a symbol of Jesus, the Light of the world (John 8:12). Christ is the Light in the midst of the church, so a local church has the presence of God there in a unique way.

Second, today's symbols of redemption are the Lord's Table and baptism, whereas the symbols of redemption in the Old Testament were the sacrifice and the furniture in the tabernacle. Baptism and the Lord's Table are local church ordinances. Christians are required to assemble where these symbols are celebrated.

Third, God's man is called to minister in the church. God calls His servants (John 15:16) and gives them gifts (Romans 12:3-8), then gives these gifted men to the church (Ephesians 4:7-13). Since God's man serves in the church, Christians should gather themselves under his ministry.

God has promised to dwell with His children anywhere (Deuteronomy 33:27); but more important, when they serve Him, God has promised to be with them (Matthew 28:20). A believer may drop to his knees by his bed and be enveloped in the love of God. God has promised, "I will never leave thee, nor forsake thee" (Hebrews 13:5).

Some extremists claim God's presence dwells only in the church. This is not so. Personal Christianity demands the presence of Christ in every believer (Galatians 2:20; Ephesians 3:17); however, His special presence is in the local church. This demands both private and corporate access to God. Private Christianity alone is unbalanced religion. To be a successful Christian, you must worship by yourself and with the church corporate.

BELONG WHERE YOU LIVE

Recently, a middle-aged school teacher walked down the aisle during the invitational hymn, saying, "I've been praying about it a long time; I want to put my membership here where I live."

The pastor looked at her in mute surprise. Finally he said, "You've been coming here for ten years. I thought you were a member."

Many Christians have their church membership somewhere other than where they live. Some leave their church membership where their parents are located. Others, wanting to get away from God, leave their church letter where it is.

Belong-where-you-live is a New Testament practice. Apollos was eloquent in the Scriptures. The church-where-he-had-been wrote a letter to the church-where-he-was-going recommending him (Acts 18:27). And he immediately became involved in the new church's ministry (Acts 18:28).

Why should you transfer your church membership when you move?

1. *The new church will watch over you.* When you join a church, you take on its obligations, which involve purity of life, service, faithfulness in attendance of services, and belief in the fundamentals of the faith. You place yourself under the teaching and preaching of the Word of God. In the past, the church's practice and belief was called *church discipline.* If a Christian did not discipline himself, he was disciplined by the congregation. By positive discipline of teaching and preaching as well as negative discipline (correction), Christians were encouraged to live for God.

When you move to a new community, you should place

yourself under the discipline of a local church. The hymn writer noted, "Prone to wander, Lord, I feel it." Since all men have a tendency to drift away from God, they need a group of people to encourage them to faithfulness. Church membership should be like food to strengthen the weak, salve to heal the oppressed, a conscience to smite the tempted, and a mother's love to encourage the child.

2. *For the influence of your testimony.* The very act of aligning yourself with a group of fundamental believers is an announcement to your new community that you plan to serve Jesus Christ.

"Why can't we wait awhile to make sure that we have the right church?" is often heard. Some like to "shop around." But you don't find a local church like you shop for a lawn mower. When a Christian moves to a new city, he should purchase a home in a suburb where there is a gospel-preaching church. Since a Christian believes the spiritual development of his family is more important than anything else, he should never locate his family where there is no gospel-preaching church.

Many people purchase a home for status, convenience, or business reasons only. But a Christian should: (1) locate near a fundamental church; or (2) plan to start a fundamental church if none is available. If a family is not strong enough to start a church, their relocation may be outside the will of God. It is never God's will for a Christian to place himself in circumstances where his spiritual life will decay. Perhaps a Christian will have to give up the business promotion that is associated with moving, or even resign from the company.

Why join another church as expediently as possible? You are a light for God. A candle gives off light immediately upon being lit, not some time later. Also, the closer you move to the candle, the brighter the light. Since a Christian wants his testimony to be brightest in his home community, he should join a church as soon as he finds a Bible-believing church with which he feels comfortable.

3. *For more effective service.* Christians who belong to a church are able to accomplish more for God. You can invite people to "your" church with enthusiasm and authority. Paul told the Colossians, "And whatsoever ye do, do it heartily, as to the Lord . . ." (Colossians 3:23). To be a whole-hearted soul-winner, you should be an enthusiastic church member.

"To attach soul-winning to church membership sounds narrow," someone might criticize. Yet, this is a Biblical teaching. First, every man is lost so every Christian is commanded to be a soul-winner to reach him (Matthew 28:19a). Christ commands every person to be baptized (Matthew 28:19b); therefore, every soul-winner ought to have his converts baptized. Since baptism places a man into the local body (Romans 6:3-4; Ephesians 1:22-23), every soul-winner ought to be a church member so he is an example of what he expects others to be. Just as you've got to have measles to spread them, every person ought to be enthusiastic about his local church so he can encourage others.

Many Christians want to teach Sunday School, work a bus route, sponsor youth organizations, or serve in some other place in the new church. If you have a gift for service, you ought to be using it for Jesus Christ. Most New Testament churches will not allow a person to serve until he is a member. While some may feel it is narrow to expect a person to be a church member before serving, there are reasons for taking that position. When a person makes a commitment to the membership of a local church, the congregation receives a commitment regarding the person's belief, life, and loyalty.

Therefore, you should prepare yourself for Christian

service by moving your membership to the new church. You moved your dog, kitchen table, bank account, and mailing address so you can live in the new town. Why not move your church membership for the same reason?

Chapter 8
Your Ultimate Step of Obedience

If baptism is the first step of obedience, the Lord's Table is the completed step. Of these two church ordinances, the Lord's Table is the most misunderstood and abused; hence, we can say many begin their first step of the Christian life but few complete God's cycle.

People have distorted ideas about the Lord's Table. The first time I served it in my student pastorate, I found the ladies at the back steps of the church pouring the grape juice on the ground.

"We thought the juice was special since it had been prayed over," the ladies told me. The were uncomfortable about pouring it back into the bottle.

In a second student pastorate, the deacons climbed over everyone's knees to serve the bread instead of passing the tray down the row. It was embarrassing for me, and when they got back to the front, I whispered, "Pass the tray from the aisle."

They were shocked and the spirit of the meeting was broken. They thought "serving" communion had more legitimacy when the "elder served the younger."

Some churches serve communion every Sunday. One church celebrated communion only once in two years, prompting a member to remind his pastor that the command of Jesus, "As oft as ye eat . . ." had become "as seldom as ye eat."

These are only a few of the misunderstandings surrounding the Lord's Table. The Roman Catholics believe the elements actually turn to the body and blood of the Lord. The Salvation Army in deep sincerity sees these abuses and refuses to celebrate communion.

Therefore, what should be your attitude as a child of God? You want to obey Christ and be the best possible Christian. Since the Lord's Table is the completed step of obedience, you will want to celebrate it as the Lord commanded, in a manner that will produce the most growth in your life.

WHY BELIEVERS SHOULD CELEBRATE COMMUNION

1. *You obey the commands of Christ.* Just as you grew spiritually when you obeyed the Lord in baptism, you will grow when you properly take communion.

One of the last acts of Jesus before His death was gathering His disciples for the first communion. He commanded, "Take, eat; this is my body" (Matthew 26:26). To make sure there was no misunderstanding, Paul repeated the command to the Corinthian church (I Corinthians 11:24).

Not only did Christ command us to remember Him,

but He said "often" (I Corinthians 11:26). The command to eat often makes us confess our sin and get cleansed often.

Regarding the Lord's Table, we come to the same conclusion we did about baptism. Celebrating communion will not make us spiritual; but if we neglect it, we can't be spiritual because we haven't obeyed our Master.

2. *You join in fellowship by communion.* Breaking bread is a natural expression of fellowship between friends. But in the Scriptures, the phrase "breaking bread" means the Lord's Table. Paul broke bread on the first day of the week (Acts 20:7), and the early Christians broke bread and fellowshipped together (Acts 2:42).

On Easter Sunday afternoon Jesus walked to Emmaus with two disciples, but they didn't recognize Him. As they sat down to eat, "he took bread, and blessed it, and brake, and gave to them. And their eyes were opened, and they knew him . . ." (Luke 24:30,31). This meal was not the Lord's Table, but the act was so well known they recognized Jesus. Just so, when we come to the communion table, we see Him with the eyes of faith. This is the ultimate communion.

When God's people sit down together at the Lord's Table, a sense of oneness is generated. At the communion table we symbolize the oneness Christ prayed that believers might have (John 17:21-23). Each person realizes he would not be there if it were not for a common salvation experience and a common love for spiritual things.

The early church had fellowship, but not as the liberal churches desire ecumenicalism. Notice the steps leading to oneness: (1) They received the word, salvation (Acts 2:41); (2) new converts were baptized, becoming a part of the local body (Acts 2:41); (3) they continued in doctrine: they studied, accepted, and tried to live the church's teaching (Acts 2:42); (4) they fellowshipped together (Acts 2:42); and finally, (5) they broke bread, the Lord's Table (Acts 2:42). The order is clear; the Lord's Table is the culmination of fellowship.

If you have never taken the Lord's Table, notice God's order and follow it closely to get His blessing. There must be fellowship of eternal life first, fellowship of joint purpose second, fellowship of doctrine third, and then you can have the intimate fellowship of communion.

You can be closer to other Christians than some brothers in the flesh. When you "abide in Christ" and let Him abide in you (John 15:1-7), you approach the closest intimacy on earth.

When I approach the Lord's Table, I confess my sins. I want nothing between my Lord and me. When I take the elements in my mouth, I once again remember taking Christ into my heart at salvation. I remember His blood and broken body were a substitute for me. At that moment I realize others are with me. They too are confessing their sins. I feel close to others because I come closer to the Lord than at any other time.

The eloquent Melvill caught the spirit of this when he said, "Inasmuch as the bread and the wine represent the body and blood of the Saviour, the administration of the ordinance is so commemorative of Christ's having been offered as a sacrifice that we seem to have before us the awful and mysterious transaction, as though the cross were again reared and the words 'It is finished' pronounced in our hearing."

Of course, we have communion with those about us, but the Lord's Table is meaningful because He is there. We talk to Him. He forgives our sins as we confess them. We commune with Christ.

3. *You examine your life and confess sin.* In earlier times, a member appeared before the pastor for examina-

tion. The church member then received a ticket to communion on the Lord's Day. But the Scriptures command, "Let a man examine himself, and so let him eat of that bread, and drink of that cup" (I Corinthians 11:28). Notice, you are to examine yourself. This is not the duty of a minister or a priest. If you are a child of God, the Holy Spirit can shine the light of His conviction upon your conscience.

The best time to examine yourself is at the beginning of the communion service. When sins come to light, do three things immediately. First, confess the sin and ask God's cleansing by the blood. "If we confess our sins, he is faithful and just to forgive us our sins, and to cleanse us from all unrighteousness" (I John 1:9). If you sincerely confess, God has promised to forgive you. So don't be afraid to take the elements.

I once met a man who had "confession-itis." He always confessed but never claimed God's forgiveness. He saw himself as a bad boy put in the corner. He continually said, "I'm sorry," but wouldn't accept his Father's forgiveness and come out of the corner. Hence, he never experienced the joy of communion at the Table.

The second step in confession is restitution. If you have wronged a brother, go to him. God will understand your motives and forgive you as you are willing to forgive him.

The third step deals with determination. Make up your mind you will not go back to the sin you have confessed. How can you eat the bread and drink the juice which symbolizes forgiveness of sin while harboring that sin in your heart?

There are two extremes which can hurt you in preparing for the Lord's Table. First, you may get too trifling with small issues and not eat. This is wrong, for Christ commands, "Let a man examine himself, and so let him eat. . . ." Mother says, "Wash your hands and come eat." She means wash as best you can (sincerity), then come to the table and eat.

The second extreme is harboring sin at the Lord's Table. Christ now warns, "For he that eateth and drinketh unworthily, eateth and drinketh damnation to himself" (I Corinthians 11:29).

The sin of the Corinthians was not the sin in their heart but in their manner of eating. They were getting drunk at the Lord's Table. Paul's rebuke of the believers begins in I Corinthians 11:17-22. He frankly stated that their coming together was more trouble than it was worth; that is, they were guilty of causing more sin than they were dealing with at communion.

By saying this, Paul partly believed what was reported to him. He probably meant to show that he did not feel all believers in Corinth were guilty of divisiveness. Paul seemed to use sarcasm when he said that there *had* to be factions (heresies) in the church in order for those approved by God to stand out sharply by contrast (I Corinthians 11:19).

Immediately following the last Passover meal with His disciples, Jesus instituted the Lord's Table. However, in Corinth the love feast had degenerated into a first-come, first-served smorgasbord. Some stuffed themselves; others got drunk. Those who were well-off financially consumed the food and drink; the poor believers who came later had nothing. With some in a stupor, and those who came late resentful, the congregation was hardly in the right spirit to experience the forgiveness of the Lord. Some had become so hardened through the Lord's Table observance that God took them home in premature death. "For this cause many are weak and sickly among you, and many sleep" (I Corinthians 11:30).

If they asked God's forgiveness, it was not sincere. I used to have an uncle who said this at the table: "Pardon our sins, and pass the biscuits . . . Amen." No one ever thought he was sincere about the sins, but we all knew he meant business about the biscuits.

4. *You praise God and give thanks.* Jesus began by giving thanks. You should do likewise, but this is more than thanking God as you do for food at each meal. You thank God for Christ's atonement. You received the greatest blessing in life because of Calvary. Therefore, Paul calls it "the cup of blessing" (I Corinthians 10:16). Next time you bow at the Lord's Table, praise God for all the blessings that have come to you because of salvation.

5. *You look forward to the Lord's second coming.* When the Lord gathered His disciples in the Upper Room for that first communion, He also promised it would be His last supper on earth. "I will not drink henceforth of this fruit of the vine, until that day when I drink it new with you in my Father's kingdom" (Matthew 26:29). Christ was pointing them to His return. Just as the elements are a *backward look* and the self-examination is an *inward look,* the Lord now points them to a *forward look.* On many communion tables you find engraved, "till he come" (I Corinthians 11:26).

During the Second World War a mother always set a place at the table for her son who was overseas. She remembered him as her little boy and it caused her sadness that he wasn't there. But its positive side gave her hope. She expected him to return. When you arise from the table, pray with John the beloved disciple, "Even so, come, Lord Jesus" (Revelation 22:20).

HOW TO CELEBRATE THE LORD'S TABLE

1. *Communion is a church ordinance.* You should not gather your family around the supper table and pass out grape juice and break bread to celebrate the Lord's Table. It is a church ordinance. The first instructions

were given to the church at Corinth, when Paul said, "For I have received of the Lord that which also I delivered unto you" (I Corinthians 11:23). The "you" referred to the church. He noted earlier, "When ye come together in the church . . ." (I Corinthians 11:18), and again, "Despise ye the church of God . . ." (I Corinthians 11:22).

The purpose of the Lord's Table is to bring communion to the local body, not a family. Also, the remembrance of His broken body symbolizes the local body into which you were baptized. Finally, those who were sinning were accused of not "discerning the Lord's body" (I Corinthians 11:29). This was in reference to their callous attitude toward the local body, the church.

2. *Communion is for baptized believers.* If you have not been properly baptized, you should not take communion. The doctrine of allowing only baptized persons to partake of communion was taught by almost all denominations until approximately 100 years ago—by Baptists, Presbyterians, Methodists, Congregationalists. However, with a general softening of doctrine by many churches has come a loosening of restrictions to the Lord's Table.

Why should a person be baptized before taking communion? First, a person can't examine himself honestly by God's Word and say he has obeyed Christ if he has not followed the first step of obedience. Second, the Great Commission gives the pattern: "Go ye therefore, and teach all nations, baptizing them . . . Teaching them to observe all things whatsoever I have commanded you" (Matthew 28:19,20). They must be won to Christ, baptized, then taught to obey Him. Included in His admonition to "observe all things whatsoever I have commanded" is His command to "eat ye all of it."

The example of the early church followed the pattern

of the Great Commission (Acts 2:41,42). By eating together, they declared themselves in partnership with doctrine, practice, and life (I Corinthians 10:16-21).

Some think the pastor displays little brotherly love if everyone is not invited to the Lord's Table. The argument is heard, "It's the Lord's Table. Why should any Christian be excluded?" The answer is simple. Those who are not obedient should not be invited to eat with the faithful.

Remember, there were some in Jerusalem who knew the Lord but they were not invited to the supper in the Upper Room. Only the disciples were present. Today, all are Christ's disciples who love Him (John 13:34,35), who continue in His Word (John 8:31), and bear fruit (John 15:8). Therefore, those disciples who meet His qualifications should come to the table. And finally, a strong point in favor of this opinion, Jesus waited until Judas left to serve the communion.

3. *Communion has a proper procedure.* In I Corinthians 11:27-32 we find a solemn warning from Paul regarding the condition of each believer's heart as he partakes of communion. Anyone eating the bread and drinking the juice unworthily will be guilty of desecrating Christ. Therefore, prior to partaking of the elements, each one is responsible before God for examining himself and confessing any sin in his life. Only then is he to take the elements with a clear conscience.

The next procedure to follow in celebration of the Lord's Table is found in I Corinthians 11:23-26. In imitation of Christ Himself, the leader in the congregation is to take bread, thank God for it, break it, and serve it to the others, reminding them that this represents the body of Christ which was broken (or given) in suffering for them. Then he is to take the cup, remind the others that this represents the blood of Christ shed for their sins, and invite them to drink from it.

In the Upper Room, the disciples ended the service by singing a hymn (Matthew 26:30). Most churches follow this example.

Since much is at stake in celebrating the Lord's Table, every precaution should be taken to make sure it goes well. Deacons and deaconesses who prepare the elements must do their work well. The pastor who presides over the table must do his work well. Those who serve the elements must do their work well. The musicians who provide music must do their work well. The members of the congregation must conduct themselves in such a way as to contribute to the proper atmosphere of the service and not do anything to detract from it.

When people do all that is expected of them, the Holy Spirit ministers in such a way that celebration of the Lord's Table can be a deeply satisfying experience. He stands ready to do this each time we meet around the Lord's Table; so let's prepare for Him and rejoice in His presence when He comes to bless us.

PART IV

Serving the Lord Successfully

Chapter 9
Victory Over Sin Is Promised You

While in high school, my buddy Art Winn and I went squirrel hunting. We were walking in the bottom of a 12-foot drainage ditch when the ditch forked in two different directions. Art took the right branch and planned to meet me about a mile away. After he left it began to rain, and I crawled under the overhanging root system of an oak tree which gave me a cave-like protection.

I lay in the dry leaves for several minutes before realizing how cold I was. Pulling some leaves together, I made a fire. In the light of the flames, I saw a black snake. Even though I knew it was non-poisonous, I scrambled out of my small cave. I enjoyed the cave until the light revealed the snake; then I wouldn't go back even to get out of the rain.

The same thing happened in my Christian life. I was comfortable with sins in my life until the light of Christ revealed them. Then I had to change, and I can't enjoy going back to the old ways.

LEARN HOW TO DEAL WITH SIN

If you are a new Christian you might have questions regarding right and wrong. Some things which you enjoyed before you were saved may now make you uncomfortable.

We will try to stay away from pronouncements naming sins, unless they are called sin in the Bible. Rather, principles will be laid down from the Word of God by which each Christian can determine what is wrong for the child of God.

1. *You must do what God directs.* The Westminster Confession of Faith asks the question, "What is sin?" The first part of the answer is, "Sin is any want of conformity . . . ." Anything that does not conform to God's Word is sin.

When a mother says to her son, "Go to the store and get bread," what should be her reaction when he disobeys? When she finds him playing baseball on the corner, she can't be happy. He has disobeyed his mother (Ephesians 6:1), and if he continues, a serious flaw will develop in his character.

There are certain commandments that are easy to obey, meaning there is no question about what the Christian should do. You are to tithe (Malachi 3:10), attend church (Hebrews 10:25), confess your sins (I John 1:9), and love other Christians (John 13:34). The same can be said for reading your Bible, praying, and watching for His second coming.

We may think the sin of omission is not as great as the sin of hardheaded disobedience. When a father asks his

12-year-old boy to wash the car and he forgets, it is not as bad as his twin brother throwing mud at the car. The father is displeased with both sons, and he deals with each offense differently. But he can't overlook the one who didn't wash the car. The Scriptures teach, "Therefore to him that knoweth to do good, and doeth it not, to him it is sin" (James 4:17).

2. *You must not do what God says is wrong.* The Ten Commandments are all negative warnings beginning, "Thou shalt not . . ." You sin when you go against God's commandments. God says it is wrong to kill, lie, steal, commit adultery, and have idols in your life (Exodus 20:3-17).

The commands of God are not grievous; He did not take away the "fun" things. Some have mistakenly thought, "All the pleasure is gone now that I am a Christian." God is not a mean father who keeps His children locked in a closet all day. Jesus said, "I am come that they might have life, and that they might have it more abundantly" (John 10:10).

But like a wise father, God knows some things will harm His children. What parents would allow their children to play near a busy highway or in a field with snakes? When God says no, don't rebel or see how close you can get to the edge. Try to see why God said no. When you understand the purpose of God, you can obey with enthusiasm.

3. *You must obey your conscience.* Your conscience is a moral regulator that flashes information to the brain. It tells you what it thinks is right and wrong. Like the thermostat upstairs, when things get chilly it starts the furnace in the basement. When your conscience tells you something is wrong, it is a sin to go against it. At birth, the conscience is pure, reflecting the image of God in which you were made. The conscience tells man it is

wrong to murder, steal and lie. You have the moral law of God branded in your heart. God recognized the moral law that He has implanted within man, and you sin when you violate your conscience.

My father was an alcoholic. I saw the misery he caused my mother. We children had to do without because he drank so heavily. I don't know if alcoholism can be communicated by influence or physical succession, but I've always had a fear of liquor of any kind.

I once refused communion because real wine was served. I will not take meat cooked in liquor in any form, even though the alcohol is burned off. My conscience tells me if I got one taste, I might become an alcoholic. Some may think I am narrow, but I believe it is sin to go against your conscience. "Therefore to him that knoweth to do good, and doeth it not, to him it is sin" (James 4:17)

While I feel it is a sin to ignore your conscience, some will tell you, "Let your conscience be your guide." This is bad advice. Your conscience cannot always be trusted. Your conscience can be "educated" to not feel the wrongness of some situations and your spiritual life will suffer.

The conscience can be "seared": "Having their conscience seared with a hot iron" (I Timothy 4:2). This pictures a hot poker burning a scab on the skin. The conscience is seared when one continually goes against its instructions.

Note the following guidelines for your conscience. First, everything your conscience tells you to do may not be right. Some people think it is allowable to steal or lie under certain conditions. Second, your conscience won't tell you everything that is wrong. The conscience depends upon the training it has received. Some people commit adultery not realizing what God has said about sexual purity.

Third, it is wrong for you to go against your conscience, even when others disagree. There are many Christians who eat flaming steaks marinated in liquor, and they may get no more alcohol than when I eat mine charcoal broiled. Marinated steaks may be acceptable to them, but for me it is wrong because I would have to go against my conscience.

Follow your conscience to a certain extent. Pray that God would enlighten it daily. But don't let your conscience be the final deciding factor in what you do for God.

4. *You must not harbor impure thoughts.* We live in a "girl watchers" age. Men enjoy thumbing through *Playboy* or walking the beaches to look at the bikinis. A lot of wives know this and say, "It's all right to window shop; just don't touch."

Sinful thoughts involve more than sex; the whole issue of lust is involved. Some men dream of money and the lust of "things" consumes their minds. Some women watch soap operas and the lust of illicit happiness eats them up.

You are supposed to have a clean mind (II Corinthians 10:4,5; 11:3); therefore, you shouldn't listen to filthy stories. Jesus said, "Whosoever looketh on a woman to lust after her hath committed adultery with her already in his heart" (Matthew 5:28); therefore, you shouldn't allow filthy thoughts to pollute your mind. This doesn't mean you won't be tempted with impure imaginations. A great evangelist once explained, "You can't be responsible if birds fly over your head, but it is your fault if they lodge in your hair."

As a man "thinketh in his heart, so is he" (Proverbs 23:7). Before Eve sinned by eating the forbidden fruit, she lusted in her mind. "But I fear, lest by any means, as the serpent beguiled Eve through his subtilty, so your minds should be corrupted from the simplicity that is in Christ" (II Corinthians 11:3). The first step toward sin is usually our minds thinking about the act. Paul tells us we should "think on these things" (Philippians 4:8) which uplift.

5. *You must not defile your body.* Some people have the attitude, "My soul lives forever . . . ignore the body." As a result, they overfeed their already fat body, stink it up like a tobacco barn, or pickle it in alcohol. You cannot separate your body from your soul until death. The way you treat your body reflects your attitude toward spiritual things and vice versa.

The little child stamps his feet, "I can do what I want." Yet the parent knows if he plays under the water heater he could receive a permanent scar. The teen sits smoking pot to experience blackouts when faced with any pressure or tension. Not being able to serve the Lord as a minister depressed him. The depression brought on more blackouts, and the cycle continued. In a final fit of depression, he committed suicide. The sin of taking his life began with the first sin of drug abuse.

6. *You must not link yourself with those who will cause you to stumble.* Your friends are important for they help to determine your outlook on life. Therefore, the Bible warns, "Be ye not unequally yoked together with unbelievers" (II Corinthians 6:14). This doesn't mean we should not work at the same store with a non-Christian or join the same club. It does mean you should not link yourself with an unsaved person in marriage or in any other way wherein his decisions will determine your Christian life.

The Bible teaches, "Come out from among them, and be ye separate, saith the Lord, and touch not the unclean thing; and I will receive you, And will be a Father unto you, and ye shall be my sons and daughters . . ." (II Corinthians 6:17-18). Don't get involved with people who will pull you down.

7. *You must not adversely influence others.* When Cain killed Abel, he asked, "Am I my brother's keeper?" Many have repeated that question, implying they are not responsible for others. However, John Donne described, "No man is an island. . . ." We live in a human community where every action is both influenced by and has an impact on others.

The Bible used the phrase *stumbling block* to teach that it is sin to harm others by our influence. Paul warns, "Take heed lest by any means this liberty of yours become a stumblingblock to them that are weak" (I Corinthians 8:9).

In many New Testament villages the meat sold in butcher shops had first been sacrificed to idols. New Christians who had previously worshiped idols refused to eat the meat because it was a compromise of their convictions. However, a few Christians thought hamburger was hamburger, ignoring the convictions of the other Christians.

Paul stated his opinion, "Neither, if we eat, are we the better; neither, if we eat not, are we the worse" (I Corinthians 8:8). However, Paul saw it was wrong to hurt other people by what he ate. "If meat make my brother to offend, I will eat no flesh" (I Corinthians 8:13). The Christian cannot do questionable things that may make others stumble into sin.

Many feel dancing is an artistic form, reflecting coordination, style, and rhythm. However, some Christians have been ensnared by lust through the power of suggestion, through touch, rhythmic beat, and tempting words. It comes down to a question of morality. Can a Christian who enjoys dancing purposely cause his brother for whom Christ died to stumble?

Recently a man's car began to sputter and lose its power. His mechanic checked out the spark plugs, fuel pump, and distributor; still he couldn't find the problem. Finally the mechanic's boss told him to blow out the fuel line. A little bit of trash was causing the problem. There was not enough grit to fill a quarter of a teaspoon, yet it was enough to make the car lose its power.

Sin is like trash in the fuel line. It makes you lose power to do the will of God and you fall into bad habits. Sin makes you irritable and keeps you from doing what you know is right.

8. *You must avoid temptation.* All Christians are tempted to sin. When you are plagued with a problem, don't think something is wrong. Paul notes, "There hath no temptation taken you but such as is common to man" (I Corinthians 10:13). As a matter of fact, when you are not tempted by sin, you are probably not doing much for God. To be victorious over temptation, avoid what you know to be temptation to you. The truly born-again person should not willfully sin.

When you yield to temptation, and it is possible that you will, you should be grieved that you have disappointed God, but don't let sin destroy your walk with Him. Apply God's prescription for restoring fellowship with Him: "If we confess our sins, he is faithful and just to forgive us our sins, and to cleanse us from all unrighteousness" (I John 1:9). Confession means to agree with God about our sins. We agree that sin is terrible and will destroy our Christian testimony. "He that covereth his sins shall not prosper . . ." (Proverbs 28:13). But notice the last part of that verse: ". . . but whoso confesseth and forsaketh them shall have mercy."

LEARN TO LIVE A RIGHTEOUS LIFE

A teenage girl stood on the ledge of a burning building.

The fireman on the hook and ladder couldn't get any closer to her than a handclasp.

He said, "You grab my arm, and I'll grab you . . . jump and trust me."

Victory over sin has the same two ingredients. You must leave sin and jump into God's arms. You can't keep rocking in a chair and pray for God to take away the dizziness you get from rocking. You must leave the rocking chair. God expects believers to live separated *from* sin and separated *unto* righteousness. It is not enough that you quit sinning; you must live a holy life. This is sometimes called the victorious Christian life. It is the basis of living the successful Christian life.

Let us think of some practical reasons for living a righteous life, which have grown out of the experiences of God's people. God gives us general principles which we must apply to real life situations.

1. *You are living righteously when your new nature controls your life.* Paul said, "Therefore if any man be in Christ, he is a new creature: old things are passed away; behold, all things are become new" (II Corinthians 5:17). This new nature is like the sap that runs in the dormant tree each spring. The new life pushes off the dead leaves.

Your old habits are like old leaves. A program to reform yourself is not enough. Counting to ten when you get angry is not God's way of victory. You have a new nature; let it flow. But that's hard because you still have your old sinful nature.

Your distaste for the things of the world will grow as you acquire a taste for spiritual things. Your taste for some habits will change immediately, while others will take longer periods of adjustment.

Even though I wasn't yet a Christian, I regularly attended a Sunday evening youth meeting as a junior boy. On several occasions we had a consecration service designed to purify our lives. We wrote our sins on small slips of paper and deposited them in a metal dish. After prayer, a candle ignited the paper, and my sins were supposedly purified by fire.

I always wrote "cursing" on my paper; and, after trying not to curse for a few days, I always went back to filthy speech. On one occasion I stood before a campfire and publicly told my friends I would quit cursing.

Two weeks later, as I was opening a bundle of papers to deliver on my news route, the wire broke and I gashed my knuckle. I cursed. My friend Art Winn made fun of my empty promise. I couldn't keep my mouth clean before I was saved, but I can say to the glory of God, I have never cursed since. This does not mean I am perfect, of course, only that I have victory over that sin.

2. *You live righteously showing gratitude to God for what Christ has done for you.* Paul wrote, "And whatsoever ye do in word or deed, do all in the name of the Lord Jesus, giving thanks to God and the Father by him" (Colossians 3:17).

You dishonor Christ if you continue to live in your old sinful habits. The Bible calls our unsaved state "children of disobedience" (Ephesians 2:2). If you cannot thank Christ for something you do, you had better avoid it. Let your appreciation to God for what He has done for you guide your actions.

3. *You live righteously by protecting yourself and your loved ones from the dangers and miseries which sin breeds.* A professor was rushed to the hospital with stomach cramps, but tests revealed nothing. A month later the entire family went to the emergency room with the same symptoms. Again they could find nothing.

A friend with whom they had gone to Mexico phoned a warning. They had both bought pottery that was not properly kiln dried. The lead paint was melting into the hot chocolate, causing sickness.

Although improperly fired pottery is not a sin, the same principle applies. Your sin may affect your family. You may not be offended by some of the "new" movies, but your teenage children may be eaten up with passion.

We can't get every evil influence out of our life, of course, because we live in an evil world, but separating ourselves from sinful practices whenever possible works toward godliness. When interceding for believers, Jesus prayed, "I pray not that thou shouldest take them out of the world, but that thou shouldest keep them from the evil"(John 17:15).

4. *You live righteously by maintaining a strong testimony for Christ.* After I was saved, I worried about some of my friends. "How can I keep myself clean?" I thought. I told one high school buddy I was sorry for the things we had done together before my salvation. He never came around me again.

A few days ago I talked with a college student who said he could beat me at pool. He wanted me to go to a "recreation room" to play a game, explaining, "It's not called a pool room anymore."

"I can't do that," I said. "If anyone sees me bending over a pool table, what will they think of me as a minister?"

The Bible demands that we "abstain from all appearance of evil" (I Thessalonians 5:22). Paul said, "I wrote unto you in an epistle not to company with fornicators: yet not altogether with the fornicators of this world, or with the covetous, or extortioners, or with idolaters; for then must ye needs go out of the world. But now I have written unto you not to keep company, if any man that is called a brother be a fornicator, or covetous, or an idolater, or a railer, or a drunkard, or an extortioner; with such an one no not to eat" (I Corinthians

5:9-11).

Believers have to maintain contact with sinners and backsliders in order to be a witness to them, but intimate association with them is discouraged. I would go in a "recreational room" to witness for Christ, but not for pleasure. I would go into a bar to witness, but not to drink a soft drink.

5. *You live righteously when your life has priorities.* If you only have a limited time for reading, do not spend it all on secular novels or magazines. Jesus said, "Seek ye first the kingdom of God" (Matthew 6:33). The first priority in your life is spiritual maturity. Read Christian books and magazines that will enrich your life. Spend time with your Bible. But this doesn't mean you shouldn't read the newspapers or other necessary items. Matthew 6:33 continues, ". . . All these things shall be added unto you." The principle is that you should use your time, money, and energy to achieve spiritual growth.

You should not support evil enterprises. Satan offers many pleasures and evil habits to people and takes their money, time, and energy to pay for them. Christians certainly ought not to be guilty of supporting any of them. A boycott of evil things is one of the most powerful ways we can show our protest against their existence and influence.

6. *You live righteously by preparing yourself for Heaven.* There will be no evil in Heaven, so separation from evil here on earth gives us a foretaste of Heaven.

The young girl stops dating other boys the minute she falls in love with her future husband. She doesn't wait until the wedding ceremony; she prepares herself to live with one man by spending time with him. You should get ready to spend all eternity with the bridegroom, Jesus Christ. If you don't like the thought of loving Him only, maybe you are not a child of God.

Paul said that if we will think about things which are true, honest, just, pure, lovely, well-reported, virtuous, and praiseworthy, and if we will put them into practice, the God of peace will be with us (Philippians 4:8,9). We need for Him to be with us until the day we go to be with Him.

Separation from this life means entrance into our life with God and Christ in Heaven. "For our conversation [citizenship] is in heaven; from whence also we look for the Saviour, the Lord Jesus Christ" (Philippians 3:20). Until that day comes, however, determine to live a pure life. Paul said, "I pray God your whole spirit and soul and body be preserved blameless unto the coming of our Lord Jesus Christ" (I Thessalonians 5:23).

MAKE VICTORY THE GOAL OF LIVING

While preaching to a small congregation in Northern Ontario, I saw a great moving of the Spirit; 27 out of a congregation of approximately 85 persons came forward, most of them for salvation.

"I've got a hideous sin in my life," one of the church leaders confessed to me at the altar. All sin is hideous in God's sight, but by human judgments, I didn't think his sin was all that terrible.

"I must have victory," he poured out his soul to God. His sincerity and agony moved me. Never had I seen a man who wanted victory over a habit more than this Sunday School teacher and soul-winner.

Do you crave spiritual victory? Maybe your honest search for God's deliverance will bring revival to your church as this man's yieldedness triggered the Spirit's movement among the unsaved. I wish every Christian wanted victory over sin as this man did. Perhaps some don't want it because they don't know what victory is and what it can do for them.

1. *Victory over spiritual laziness.* There are times when you just don't want to read the Bible. Yet you know you *should.* You are spiritually lazy. What should you do? You should do *right.* Read your Bible. The same thing happens with prayer. You are spiritually lazy and you say, "I don't want to pray, but I'm supposed to pray so I will." Leave your lazy nature and go to the prayer closet and force yourself to pray. Spiritual victory is getting your lazy nature to obey your spiritual nature.

2. *Victory over materialism.* When you follow the commands of God, He will supply your needs: money, clothes, or food. We are all familiar with Psalm 23:1: "The Lord is my shepherd; I shall not want [for anything I need]." David also wrote, "I have been young, and now am old; yet have I not seen the righteous forsaken, nor his seed [children] begging bread" (Psalm 37:25). Paul said, "My God shall supply all your need according to his riches in glory by Christ Jesus" (Philippians 4:19).

One of the reasons we bow our heads at the beginning of a meal and give thanks is because God provides our needs. A few people are rich and have no needs. Most everyone else has needs of all kinds. A Christain looks to God to supply these. He must join the vast majority who bow their heads and ask God for money, food, clothes, or shelter.

3. *Victory over ignorance.* When God offered King Solomon whatever he wanted, Solomon asked for wisdom, and God gave it to him (I Kings 3:5-12). In Isaiah 55:8,9 we read that God's thoughts and ways are as high above man's as the Heavens are above the earth; yet in Psalm 32:8 we hear God's promise to man: "I will instruct thee and teach thee in the way which thou shalt go: I will guide thee with mine eye."

In the Old Testament, God taught men through visions, dreams, angels, seers, prophets, priests, and various agencies. In the New Testament, God sent His Son to teach men, and upon His return to Heaven Christ sent the Holy Spirit to guide us into all truth (John 16:13). God gave us His Word by inspiration of the Holy Spirit (II Peter 1:21), and we are instructed in doctrine and the way of living righteously by reading and studying it: "All scripture is given by inspiration of God, and is profitable for doctrine, for reproof, for correction, for instruction in righteousness: That the man of God may be perfect, throughly furnished unto all good works" (II Timothy 3:16,17).

Chapter 10
Knowing God's Will for Your Life

God has a purpose for your life. You cannot be a successful Christian if you miss His plan. The plan of God is usually called the will of God. When a father tells his son, "Go to the store," that is the father's will.

God has a place for you to live, a person for you to marry, and a job for you to do. The will of God concerns these large decisions. But what about small decisions?

A zealous college freshman stood in a department store considering two shirts. He had money for only one. "Which shirt is the will of God for me?" he asked his friend who laughed at him. Is God's plan so specific that it includes what color shirt we buy?

But not all decisions Christians make are in the will of God. A missionary returned home from the field in broken health. He had worked so diligently that he had not eaten or slept properly; yet friends said it was the will of God for him to come home. Can we blame God when we break the laws of nutrition and call the consequences the will of God?

Two high school boys wanted to preach the gospel and win souls. They went to the slums, rented a house, and called it a church. They nailed up a church sign and visited the neighbors; yet the experiment lasted only one month. They were sincere and worked hard, but they failed. They thought they were in the will of God. Can we force our decisions on God and call them His will? Obviously, God would not call high school boys to start a church.

LEARNING ABOUT GOD'S WILL

You can look to Jesus as your example in finding the will of God. His entire life was dedicated completely to the Father's will. He once said, "My meat is to do the will of him that sent me . . ." (John 4:34). Again He prayed, "Not my will, but thine, be done" (Luke 22:42). Doing the will of God is simply doing what God wants you to do. When Jesus taught us to pray, "Thy will be done," it means we will do what God expects.

1. *God's will is knowable.* The Psalmist said, "The meek will he guide in judgment: and the meek will he teach his way" (Psalm 25:9). Every man can find God's will. Every man! Not just full-time preachers, but everyone. Even the little boy in the first grade should be taught that God wants him to develop his abilities and grow as Jesus did.

God expects us to know and do His will. Paul exhorted, "Be ye not unwise, but understanding what the will of the Lord is" (Ephesians 5:17). Two facts arise from this verse: first, the will of God can be understood;

and second, those who do not know the will of God are not wise. Some search for the will of God like looking through a ring of keys, using the trial and error method. But God does not hide His will like the miser hiding his money.

2. *God shows His will to those who will do it.* The week's groceries won't hop off the grocery shelves and place themselves on the table. Before you can eat you must get a job and work diligently; then you use your earnings to purchase groceries. Even when you get your food to the house, it must be prepared. Laziness is inconsistent with God's will.

The will of God will not be forced on the unyielded Christian. God's will is revealed only to those who wholly desire it. We have to be sure that our will, heart, affections, and desires are wholly surrendered to Him.

The student who wants to write the best term paper spends endless hours in the library researching material. Just so, the Christian who wants the perfect will of God must search for it with his whole heart. Paul noted, "I beseech you therefore, brethren, by the mercies of God, that ye present your bodies a living sacrifice . . . that ye may prove what is that good, and acceptable, and perfect, will of God" (Romans 12:1,2). The word *present* means to give. The father who gives a bicycle to his young boy has yielded it for his son's use. You must yield your life to find the will of God and be available for His use.

Almost every man in the world has driven a nail with his shoe. When his wife asks, "Hang this picture," he looks for the nearest thing at hand because he doesn't want to go to the basement for a hammer. He drives the nail with his shoe because it's available. God doesn't walk only through the universities looking for the polished hammer with a PhD. God is looking for available people. Any young person who is willing to do anything can be used of God. Dwight L. Moody had an eighth grade education, but he shook America with one hand and Great Britain with the other because he was willing to do anything that God wanted.

3. *God's will is good for us.* Some young people will not surrender to God, thinking they will be miserable if they do. A girl remembers being embarrassed in speech class and resists becoming a missionary. A boy makes fun of a preacher and later is afraid to work on the Sunday School buses, thinking people will mock him.

In Romans 12:1,2, just quoted, Paul reminds us that the will of God is good. We don't have to prove to God that His will is good. He knows that. We must prove it to ourselves. We prove God's will by yielding ourselves to Him and following His revealed will.

When Paul's friends feared for his life but could not persuade him to stay away from Jerusalem, they said, "The will of the Lord be done," and they left the matter in God's hands (Acts 21:14). That is all we can do sometimes, and that is enough in such situations. If God's will is done, the right thing will be done.

4. *God's will is expressed in His laws.* A missionary pilot was told by the Canadian aviation authorities there was a storm coming. Yet he had an important meeting two hours away: the council was placing all missionaries for the coming three years. He took off anyway and was killed in a snowstorm.

"Lord, we don't understand Your will; we only accept it," was prayed at his funeral. Many asked why God took him. That was a wrong question. God directs some activities and permits others. God did not direct the missionary's death. The missionary broke the laws of aviation and of nature.

You cannot go contrary to the laws of God (whether in Scripture or nature) and not suffer consequences. A man falling out of a tree can't pray for God to keep him from breaking a leg. He must yield to the consequences and ask God to work through the circumstances.

The will of God should not be a dumping ground for personal failures. The missionary who had broken the laws of health and nutrition suffered the consequences. The missionary in the plane had broken the laws of nature and suffered the consequences. God could have performed one of two miracles (the supernatural transcending of the laws of nature): He could have caused the plane to ride out the snowstorm, or God could have raised the missionary from the dead. Some felt God should have guided him through the storm, but none expected him to be raised from the dead.

When you seek the will of God for your life, don't expect Him to go against His laws. God works *through* His laws (sowing and reaping, working for money, tithing) to perform His will. Some have asked for God to supernaturally provide money; but they haven't worked, nor have they tithed. Maybe this is why God has not answered their prayer.

The Holy Spirit will guide you into the will of God when the Bible is not specific. "For as many as are led by the Spirit of God, they are the sons of God" (Romans 8:14). The Holy Spirit doesn't speak in audible words. Stay away from people who hear voices from God. But the Holy Spirit can lead through your desires. If you are yielded, what you want to do may be God's will for you. "Delight thyself also in the Lord; and he shall give thee the desires of thine heart" (Psalm 37:4). Then the Holy Spirit gives us power to make our desires a realization.

5. *God's will is personal.* He is interested in all your ordinary personal activities. Don't be afraid to say, "Lord, I'll do Your will whatever it is." He will not put you on the wrong airplane or make you marry the wrong person

when you are willing to follow His direction. He won't even let you starve or go without a place to sleep. His will concerns your vacations, business trips, or a spin to the shopping center. These fall within the larger context of God's will for your life. Paul said he hoped to go to Rome by the will of God (Romans 1:10; cf 15:32). He said he would go to Corinth "shortly, if the Lord will" (I Corinthians 4:19).

James spelled out God's will regarding the details of life in no uncertain terms, when he said, "Go to now, ye that say, To day or to morrow we will go into such a city, and continue there a year, and buy and sell, and get gain: Whereas ye know not what shall be on the morrow. For what is your life? It is even a vapour, that appeareth for a little time, and then vanisheth away. For that ye ought to say, If the Lord will, we shall live, and do this, or that" (James 4:13-15).

6. *God's will is that we be successful.* God never planned for you to fail. He wants us to overcome temptation (I Corinthians 10:13) and to overcome the world (I John 5:4). When we are victorious, we endure. "And the world passeth away, and the lust thereof: but he that doeth the will of God abideth for ever" (I John 2:17).

A defeated Christian cannot be in God's will. He is living in the flesh. We should overcome our foibles and problems. The basis for victory is the death of Christ. Paul said that Christ "gave himself for our sins, that he might deliver us from this present evil world, according to the will of God and our Father" (Galatians 1:4).

MAKING DECISIONS IN GOD'S WILL

As a new Christian you will want to do God's will. You will be faced with many decisions. Some of these will be difficult to make. You will want to make the right choice, but the alternatives are not always easy.

When you were a child, you did the will of your parents. Sometimes you didn't understand why you were doing what they wanted, but you did it anyway. At other times you did know what they wanted.

Some people have a difficult time making decisions because they are confused about God's will. Other people seem to always make the right choices. Why? Because they know the principles for finding God's will for their life. The following principles will help you make wise decisions as a Christian.

1. *Commit yourself to doing God's will.* A phrase was lettered on a large poster in the dining room at Ben Lippen camp when I worked there as a young man: THE LORD HAS A PLAN FOR YOU. God spoke to me through that poster and convinced me He had something for me. I began to actively seek His plan for my life.

The first step in knowing God's will is knowing yourself. You must want to do God's will with all your heart. God speaks to servants who aggressively seek to know His will: "If any man willeth to do his will, he shall know . . ." (John 7:17, paraphrased from the Scofield Reference Bible note).

You must actively turn your will over to God and decide to do His will before He will show it to you. You can't pray, "Lord, what is your will so I can think it over?" You can't bargain with God as did Jacob. Some don't know God's will because they are not ready to do it. God knows their heart; so He doesn't waste energy showing them what He knows they will not do.

Total commitment involves presenting your whole self—body, soul and spirit—to God, and He will show you what is His good, and acceptable, and perfect will of God (Romans 12:1,2).

2. *Look for God's will in the Bible.* The Word of God is the most vital element in finding the will of God. Read

your Bible and saturate yourself with its principles. Those who know the Bible will usually experience the leadership of God in their lives. A wise grandfather once observed, "A Bible that is falling apart usually belongs to a person who isn't." It is never the slave's job to guess what his master wants him to do. It is the master's job to speak, and the servant's job to obey. If you do not know the Bible, you will guess at God's will.

You will find that the vast majority of problems that Christians have concerning the will of God are answered in the Word of God. There are some things we shouldn't even pray about because we often use prayer as a crutch to explain our unwillingness to obey. We shouldn't pray about whether it is God's will for us to tithe or to be baptized. We should do it because it is the will of God as expressed in the Word of God. It would be ridiculous to pray whether it is God's will to take something that belongs to another. The Holy Spirit will never lead us contrary to the Word of God. He is its author and cannot deny Himself or contradict His Word.

3. *Pray for guidance in knowing God's will.* Many Christians want to tell the Lord how to solve their problems. But it is better to let Him decide how best to handle our problems, then sit back and let Him work. God's will does not operate when our will is getting in the way.

The daughter of a minister lost her contact lens on a shag carpet in the family room. The family members got down on their knees but could not find it. When the preacher realized it would cost $30 to replace the lens, he offered a $10 reward. Still they couldn't find it. The next morning the minister's wife prayed, "Jesus, You know where that lens is; lead me to it." As she prayed, the middle cushion on the couch came to her mind. When she looked under it, the lens was there.

4. *Make sure your motives are pure in seeking God's*

will. Jesus noted, "The light of the body is the eye: if therefore thine eye be single, thy whole body shall be full of light" (Matthew 6:22). The word *single* means to look only one way. We must have an eye single for the glory of God. When self becomes involved, our eyes become blurry, and we miss the glory of God. God won't hear our prayers when we harbor secret impure motives.

In a recent Miss America pageant, a contestant was asked what she wanted to achieve. "I'd like to be happy . . . that's all." The will of God was never that you be happy, but rather that you be holy. The Constitution guarantees you the right to happiness, but those who seek it never find it. There is nothing wrong with being happy, but happiness is a by-product of holiness. As a goal unto itself, it doesn't work.

John Wesley said of his early Methodists, "I'm not sure they understand love. They come to church to enjoy their religion rather than to get holiness." God wants us to enjoy our religion, but that is never our aim; it is the result. Our aim is to seek God's will because it is our duty.

5. *Do what you know is right.* God gave you certain mental equipment to use, and surely He expects you to employ your mind under the guidance of the Holy Spirit to figure out most routine problems on your own. If the mind is being constantly upgraded by renewing, we should have an easier time doing God's will. "But be ye transformed by the renewing of your mind, that ye may prove what is that good, and acceptable, and perfect, will of God" (Romans 12:2). Simply put, the will of God is doing what you know is right.

6. *Face your own thoughts, strengths, and weaknesses realistically.* It is God's will that you work in your areas of strength rather than in your areas of weakness. If you cannot sing well enough to be a soloist, join a choir. If

you aren't even good enough for that and you still love music, take up an instrument. Don't waste time and people's patience by trying to develop a career in an area of weakness. Put your time and energy on something you can do successfully.

7. *You must have peace about your decisions.* Paul said, "Let the peace of God rule in your hearts" (Colossians 3:15). To claim to know God's will about something and yet be wracked by inner turmoil about that decision is ridiculous. The peace of God floods the heart and mind of a believer once God's will is revealed, and it passes all human understanding (Philippians 4:7). It may be that God wants you to do something extremely difficult or dangerous; yet, His peace will be given to you as you face it.

If God has led you to your present position, don't change until you have peace about the move. A pastor was called to two new churches within the same week. The more he prayed, the more anxious he became. He set Saturday midnight as a deadline to make the decision, but he grew more perplexed as the deadline approached. The decision was clear; both alternatives were wrong, and he stayed where he was. If you are not absolutely confident of a new change, stay where you have peace.

A Christian once said, "Every time I'm nervous about a decision and do it anyway, it is usually the wrong decision." Paul tells us to always act out of confidence or faith: "Whatsoever is not of faith is sin" (Romans 14:23).

8. *Seek spiritual counsel from godly people.* Godly people don't necessarily have to be your pastor or his wife, although you might go to them first. You can go to anyone who walks close to the Lord and has learned how to let God guide his life. Talking over decisions with him and praying with him can give new insight to handling

problems. "Where no counsel is, the people fall: but in the multitude of counsellors there is safety" (Proverbs 11:14).

9. *Study circumstances to see whether doors are open or closed.* It seems foolish to pound on closed doors and overlook the fact that open doors are available; yet many believers do this. Even the open doors may lead to difficulties, but if it is God's will to go through them, that is the way to go. Paul said, "A great door and effectual is opened unto me, and there are many adversaries" (I Corinthians 16:9).

Opportunities are tied to the will of God. Many good things may come into your life; these may be the will of God. While a college scholarship may be God's provision for a young person's education, being born to well-to-do parents may be God's provision for the next student. Still another student may have to work his way through college and, in the process, learn the lesson of sacrifice. Each opportunity comes from God.

Watch out for opportunities, though; not all may be God's will. Not every opportunity, no matter how attractive, may be good for you and God's will is always good for you. Our desires might influence our understanding of God's will. For instance, a marriage proposal is not God's will if the young man will pull the young lady away from God. Test opportunities first by the Scriptures.

10. *Do not move forward until you know you are obeying the Bible.* When you follow God's leadership, you know where you are going. The phrase "blind faith" is often misapplied. To make a decision because you are frustrated is not faith. Neither is it faith to step off on your own inclination.

Faith is obedience to the Word of God and you should never be blind in your knowledge of the Bible. You must have open eyes to your circumstances as well as to God's

Word. Your mind must understand the consequences. God doesn't lead out of a vacuum; He leads out of full knowledge.

A Bible college student refused to work for a living. He maintained he must live by "faith." His wife left him to seek help elsewhere because their baby was starving. His was not faith but stupidity. The Bible specifically states that if a man will not work, neither shall he eat. It also says for a man to provide for his household.

Wait for God's will. Sometimes the more haste we make, the less speed we generate. He who waits on God loses no time.

11. *Judge decisions by the long look.* The Christian has eternity in his eye. He judges every opportunity by God's scale. The will of God will never shortchange you. It is not God's will for you to be ignorant when you can get an education. It is not God's will for a church to step backwards when it can reach out to the lost.

God is more concerned about your character than your circumstances. At times God will give you an easy time; rejoice. At other times He will lead you through deep waters; still rejoice. It is God's will that you become like His Son. "And be not conformed to this world: but be ye transformed by the renewing of your mind, that ye may prove what is that good, and acceptable, and perfect, will of God" (Romans 12:2).

12. *Be flexible about past decisions you have made regarding the will of God.* Too many believers have the idea that once God shows them His will, they must never change. The opposite may be true in some cases; for the will of God is not time-frozen, but cumulative. It builds up layer upon layer in the lives of most Christians.

The longer you follow the leading of the Lord, the more sensitive you will become to His will. You'll have more success in life. You'll find your life beautiful. You'll find yourself in constant conversation with the Lord. For instance, when you are witnessing to a person, and he presents an argument you may pray, "Lord, show me how to answer him."

A friend of mine who gets up while it is still dark prays, "Lord, show me the light switch." Then he remarks to whoever is within hearing distance, "If you laugh at my praying for small things, you deserve a stubbed toe."

These are twelve ways to find God's will. John Wesley, the English evangelist, said that knowing God's will is a combination of Scripture, reason, and experience. Hopefully these points have underscored that opinion.

MISSING GOD'S WILL

Before leaving this important subject, we want to deal briefly with the problem of missing the will of God. It may be that, in some situations, God's best for a person can slip by him but then be recaptured. In other situations, the opportunity may be lost forever.

1. *The unsaved who misses God's will.* Let's first think of the sinner who learns that it is God's will for him to be saved but who resists the convicting power of the Holy Spirit and remains outside of Christ. Unless he gets to the place where he no longer feels the claims of Christ, he can still be salvaged. His life may be a disaster; but if he yields to Christ, even in his dying moments, he can be saved for all eternity.

2. *The believer who resists God's will.* Then let's think of the believer who discovers God's will for him in some area of his life, but who resists the Spirit's leading and remains outside of God's will on that matter. One danger is that he will backslide and get out of fellowship with God. Another is that he will let his opportunity go by and never find it again.

A young girl was called to be a missionary but rebelled.

Much later in life she yielded and God gave her a son that surrendered to go to the mission field. The second joy was great, but only Heaven's records will show what she missed by not going herself.

If you feel you have missed an important decision in God's will for you, there is cleansing and forgiveness. God can still use you. It is never too late to do God's will. Pray much. Yield completely. God will accept your best for the rest of your life, regardless of what you might have to sacrifice to obtain it.

Chapter 11
Getting God's Power for Service

When I was nineteen years old, I pastored the Westminister Presbyterian Church, Savannah, Georgia. From eight ladies and a handful of children, the church grew to an attendance of over 100 in Sunday School.

Two blocks away another church conducted a noisy meeting with shouting and speaking in tongues every Friday evening. They could be heard two blocks away. One afternoon four men from that church came to visit me.

"We've come to pray with you and help you get the Holy Ghost," the spokesman said. They flattered me, saying the hand of God was upon my life.

"You can be greater than Billy Graham," they told me, "if you get the baptism of the Holy Ghost and speak in tongues." Being an uninformed Christian, I couldn't dispute them on an intellectual level. I wanted everything God had for me, yet I knew in my heart that they were wrong.

Over a period of years I have studied carefully the Scriptures regarding the filling of the Holy Spirit. The Holy Spirit fills His servants to win souls and to serve Him. Speaking in tongues is not an evidence of nor qualification for the filling of the Spirit.

Paul exhorts the believers, "And be not drunk with wine, wherein is excess; but be filled with the Spirit" (Ephesians 5:18). Since God commanded a Christian to be filled with the Spirit, everyone should seek it. But many Christians are confused and fearful about the filling; they are afraid to seek it.

Ephesians 5:18 tells that it is wrong to get drunk, which is being controlled by the "spirits in the bottle." When a man is drunk, the "spirits from the bottle" control his walk, his talk, and his eyesight. When a man is filled with the Holy Spirit, he is controlled by the Holy Spirit. Therefore, his walk, talk, and sight should be controlled by the Holy Spirit.

When Dr. A. J. Gordon was filled with the Spirit, he prayed, "Be thorough with me, Lord . . . be thorough." He wanted God to point out every small flaw that prevented a godly walk. Gordon built a great church because he wanted the Holy Spirit to influence every part of his life.

D. L. Moody was walking the streets of New York when he felt an urgent need for prayer. Borrowing a room from a friend, he prayed for two days lest the power of God should smite him dead. Dwight L. Moody was filled with the Spirit and shook two continents for God because the Holy Spirit completely controlled him.

When Christmas Evans sought the filling of the Holy Spirit, he wrote a 13-point covenant with God. Evans told

God what he would do if filled by the Spirit. Because of his sincerity, Evans was filled with power, and revival came to all of Wales. Curtis Hutson once said, "I wanted the fullness of the Holy Spirit more than I wanted to live." As a result, Hutson was able to influence many lives through his preaching.

When you read of the experiences of great men, be encouraged. What God has done for them, He can do for you. But be careful; don't let the experiences of others be your guide. When you seek the filling of the Holy Spirit, don't attempt to imitate their experiences, such as writing a covenant or praying for two days. Follow the principles of Scripture.

THE HOLY SPIRIT'S POWER IN YOU

The Holy Spirit is the power you need to live for God. The Holy Spirit will make you holy and spiritual. He will give you the ability to overcome a nasty temper or depression. He will help you win souls. The Bible is very clear on the teaching of the Holy Spirit. Study it carefully.

1. *The Holy Spirit indwells every believer.* When you were saved, the Holy Spirit came into your life. Most people picture salvation as asking Christ to come into their life, but at salvation the Father and the Spirit also enter the heart. As a result, the Holy Spirit dwells in every believer. "And because ye are sons, God hath sent forth the Spirit of his Son into your hearts, crying, Abba, Father" (Galatians 4:6). Actually, the Scriptures teach, "Now if any man have not the Spirit of Christ, he is none of his" (Romans 8:9). If you don't have the Holy Spirit, you are not saved.

When the Christians at Corinth sinned, Paul did not threaten them saying, "If you sin, you will lose your salvation." When Paul saw sin in the lives of Christians, he was shocked. "What? know ye not that your body is the temple of the Holy Ghost which is in you, which ye have of God . . ." (I Corinthians 6:19). His message was, "Quit sinning because you have the Holy Spirit." He indwells all believers, no matter how carnal.

The evidence that a person has the Holy Spirit living in him is seen in his actions. For the fruit of the Spirit—the results of having the Holy Spirit in one—is "love, joy, peace, long-suffering, gentleness, goodness, faith, meekness, temperance [self-control] . . ." (Galatians 5:22,23).

2. *The Holy Spirit will never leave you.* Jesus promised to send us the Holy Spirit: "I will pray the Father, and he shall give you another Comforter, that he may abide with you for ever" (John 14:16). The word *for ever* is applied to individual Christians. Paul repeats this truth when he tells the Ephesians to quit sinning because it irritates the Holy Spirit: "And grieve not the holy Spirit of God, whereby ye are sealed unto the day of redemption" (Ephesians 4:30).

Obviously, you cannot lose your salvation because of sin; He will dwell in you until the second coming of Christ: ". . . ye were sealed with that holy Spirit of promise, Which is the earnest of our inheritance until the redemption of the purchased possession . . ." (Ephesians 1:13,14). Your iniquity, however, grieves the Holy Spirit.

Once a friend mentioned that he was seeking the Holy Spirit. "I've fasted . . . tarried . . . and thirsted according to the Bible. Why can't I get the Holy Spirit?" The sincerity of his question was evident.

I told him, "The Holy Spirit is in you and He will not leave you. The Holy Spirit is a person who wants to control your life more than you want the flesh to control you. You've already got Him in your heart; now yield to Him so you can realize the potential that is yours."

The Holy Spirit is like the full tank of fuel in an

automobile, just waiting to be ignited. But somewhere between the tank and the engine there is trash in the fuel line. To blame the Holy Spirit for our empty lives is like blaming the full tank of gas in a car because the engine won't run. We have the fuel of the Holy Spirit in our hearts; now let's allow Him to work so we can get going for God.

3. *The Holy Spirit is a person, not a substance.* Many Christians treat the Holy Spirit like a substance that can be poured into a glass. The Holy Spirit is a person. Also, some treat the Holy Spirit like a ubiquitous spirit, such as the spirit of communism or the spirit of Americanism; but the Holy Spirit is a person.

When Ananias and Sapphira sinned, Peter charged them, "Thou hast not lied unto men, but unto God" (Acts 5:4). The Holy Spirit is called "He" when Christ prophesied, "He shall glorify me: for he shall receive of mine, and shall shew it unto you" (John 16:14). When the Holy Spirit comes into our lives, we have a new person within us.

Recently, I was in a room when a congressman entered. All conversation immediately silenced, and we rose. Men walked over and shook the congressman's hand; others stood and watched him. The power of the congressman's personality dominated the room. In the same way, the power of the Holy Spirit should dominate our lives. We could have ignored the congressman and gone on with our conversation, but he was so important that we couldn't. In the same way, Christians can ignore the influence of the Holy Spirit, but it grieves Him (I Thessalonians 5:19), and He should be so important in our lives that we couldn't ignore His leading.

HOW TO BE FILLED WITH THE SPIRIT

We are never commanded in the Bible to be indwelt or

sealed or baptized with the Spirit—these are all gifts from God to the believer at the moment of salvation. We are commanded, however, to be filled with the Spirit (Ephesians 5:18). To be filled with the Spirit is for the believer to allow the Spirit who lives in him to control his life. This is a matter of continuous surrender of one's life to the Spirit's control. The first step to Spirit power is desire. You begin by wanting to be filled with the Spirit. God will not force His Spirit on you or anyone else. Just as the old adage maintains, "You can lead a horse to water, but you can't make him drink," the same is true of the Christian. The filling of the Spirit will not be forced upon you.

1. *Thirsting.* When you desire the filling of the Spirit, it is the same as thirsting. Jesus described the process, "If any man thirst, let him come unto me, and drink . . . this spake he of the Spirit, which they that believe on him should receive" (John 7:37,39).

2. *Yielding.* This is the surrendering of one's will to the Spirit. When a young girl receives a proposal of marriage, she says yes if she wants the man. But that initial yes doesn't guarantee marital happiness. The couple must work at it. She must daily submit to the demands of marriage, just as the husband must.

The *yes* of submission to God's will must be followed by a daily yes to Christ, who keeps you in the center of God's will. The child of God prays, "Today I give myself to Thee to be what You want, to go where You lead, and to speak what You command."

Once you have made this prayer, you can expect Satan to mock and tempt you. It is one thing to surrender, but another to stay surrendered. Satan will say, "You didn't mean it," or "Things are going so poorly that God has forgotten about you." You may have gone to the altar and surrendered to God, yet after you left the church, you slipped into sin again. It is not God's fault that you slipped into sin. Don't blame Him. Surrendering is only the beginning of the surrendered life. You must make up your mind to always do God's will.

You need to keep an attitude of surrender. When I go downtown, I don't have to make a decision every time I come to a stop light; I just stop. I know that if I run a red light, it is dangerous, or I might get a ticket. Stopping at the red light has become an attitude of life for me.

The surrendered life takes the same approach to sin. Every time you face temptation, don't debate the merits of drunkenness, stealing, or adultery—or whatever sin the temptation may involve. When you first say yes to God, you make up your mind that you will serve Him. Now, when temptations come, rely on that attitude. Don't entertain evil desires. Obey God's traffic signals found in the Scriptures. Stopping at the signal is another way of daily saying yes to God and letting the Holy Spirit stay in control.

3. *Asking.* If you want God's power you must ask for it. Jesus spoke the parable of the pleading neighbor who came at night when his friend was in bed. Jesus commands us to "Ask, and it shall be given you; seek, and ye shall find; knock, and it shall be opened unto you" (Luke 11:9). Then Jesus explains what we should pray for: "How much more shall your heavenly Father give the Holy Spirit to them that ask him?" (Luke 11:13).

If you are defeated, ask God to give you victory. If you have never won a soul to Christ, ask God to fill you with the Spirit so you can serve Him with power.

Some go forward during the invitational hymn. They yield at the altar and ask God to fill them with the Holy Spirit. Others might bow their head as they study their Sunday School lesson and pray, "God, fill me with the Holy Spirit so I can teach this lesson as You would teach it." Still another Christian might kneel beside his bed during devotions and ask for power to overcome an explosive temper.

There are different circumstances in the filling of the Holy Spirit, but the only power is in His person. There are different methods in seeking the Holy Spirit, but one pattern given in Scripture to get it. Don't seek the experience; ask for the filling of the person of the Holy Spirit, and God will answer your prayer.

USING YOUR GIFTS IN GOD'S SERVICE

Every Christian should be serving God according to the spiritual gifts he has been given at the time of his or her new birth. Paul tells us, "Every man hath his proper gift of God . . ." (I Corinthians 7:7). And Peter repeats the same truth: "As every man hath received the gift, even so minister the same one to another . . ." (I Peter 4:10).

"If I could sing like her, I'd serve the Lord," is an often heard excuse. People envy the gifts of others yet have little concept of their own gifts. Many would like to play beautiful offertories in church, yet they are not willing to practice three hours a day for years.

"Preaching is not my gift," a young high school boy told his Sunday School teacher. "You should not preach unless you are called." There was no desire in his heart to be a minister.

"Everybody ought to be able to preach," announced the pastor from the pulpit. Which one is right? The confusion about spiritual gifts abounds, yet Paul exhorts, "Now concerning spiritual gifts, brethren, I would not have you ignorant" (I Corinthians 12:1).

A spiritual gift is a Spirit-given ability to serve God. There are three composite lists of these gifts in the Bible: Romans 12:6-8; I Corinthians 12:28-30; and Ephesians 4:11.

Beginning in Matthew 25:14, Jesus tells the parable of

the talents. One servant was given five talents, another two, and the last was given one. These talents were given "to every man according to his several ability . . ." (25:15). A talent, which was a measure of silver, represented a man's ability. We don't all have the same spiritual gifts.

In the parable, the man who used his talents faithfully received others. Perhaps you have three talents: teaching, giving money, and administration; or you could have more than three talents. God expects you to do the very best you can with the talents you have.

Every talent gets different results. Paul places them in order, noting, "God hath set some in the church, first apostles, secondarily prophets, thirdly teachers . . ." (I Corinthians 12:28). The fact that the gifts are numbered means that some are more important (or more effective) than others.

The natural question you may ask is, "How can I find my spiritual gift?"

1. *Your gifts are the work of the Holy Spirit through you.* A spiritual gift may be a natural ability with the Holy Spirit working through it. Paul describes a spiritual gift as "the manifestation of the Spirit . . ." (I Corinthians 12:7).

A young lady may sing beautifully with all the training that a rich natural voice displays, yet make no spiritual impact on the hearers. The next young lady might have a simple voice with little training, yet when she sings the Holy Spirit draws people closer to Christ. The first girl does not have a spiritual gift, whereas the second one does.

Your spiritual gifts are manifested when you are filled with the Spirit (Ephesians 5:17,18); this allows the Holy Spirit to work through you. Those who are filled have separated themselves from sin and yielded their lives for service.

2. *You were given embryonic gifts when you were saved.* Many things happened in your life when you received Jesus Christ. One of them was that the Holy Spirit came into your life to give you abilities to serve God. The giving of gifts is associated with salvation. "When he [Christ] ascended up on high, he led captivity captive, and gave gifts unto men" (Ephesians 4:8). This verse is tied with the resurrection, the point of victory over death. In that victory Christ gave abilities to His followers so that they, in turn, could be victorious in service.

At the moment of your salvation, gifts were placed in your heart, although they were not fully developed.

A pastor looking out on a group of teenagers doesn't know which one will be a missionary, doctor, accountant, or housewife. They all have different gifts for potential service. Some will find God's will and serve Christ effectively; others will choke out their spiritual strength. Since you have spiritual gifts, pray for wisdom to develop them.

3. *You find your spiritual gifts by seeking them.* The Bible teaches that your gifts grow as you seek them. "But covet earnestly the best gifts" (I Corinthians 12:31). God would not give you what is impossible; but He gives the ability and the option to seek greater power and usability.

The first step in being used of God is to volunteer for service. This is more than surrendering to His will; you must actively seek His blessing on your service. A missionary once told God, "I'm going to the mission field unless You run a train over me to stop me." The missionary had set his face to serve God abroad and would do so unless God stopped him.

On the other hand, Dr. Curtis Hutson, evangelist and former pastor of Forrest Hills Baptist Church, Decatur, Georgia, had a different prayer: "God, I believe You are calling me. If you are, keep the urge growing. If not, let it die away."

Curtis was a layman, preaching on the weekends and delivering mail on Route 41 in Decatur, when he read that Dr. Jack Hyles had baptized over 500 people. Hutson decided to go hear Hyles preach.

At that service, Hutson decided to build a church in Georgia as big as Dr. Hyles had built in Hammond, Indiana. Hutson's church grew from an attendance of approximately fifty people to over 3,000 weekly.

Your success in God's service begins with your dreams. You may never build a great church, but you can be used of God. The secret is desire. What do you want to accomplish for the Lord? You should have great dreams of doing things for God. You may never do all you dream, but you will never do more than you dream.

Some go through life and never win a soul. Others never teach a Sunday School class. Some will stand before God with little in their hands. This does not mean that God has overlooked them in giving out abilities. God will use a Christian to the degree he places himself at the disposal of the Divine. The choice is with *you,* not God. If you will meet God's qualifications, you can win great battles.

You may consider yourself too small, but you can win battles, as David defeated Goliath. You may consider yourself too old but you can be influential, as eighty-year-old Moses who brought Egypt to her knees. You may consider yourself too insecure but God's power can anoint you as it did for Gideon, the youngest son from the least family of the smallest tribe. Gideon set 130,000 Midianites to rout with 300 men.

4. *Your abilities are developed under the influence of the Bible.* The Word of God is the most important item on earth. It is more important than preachers, churches,

or Sunday School buses, for without the Bible, there is no Christianity. If you want to be used of God, you must love the thing that is the basis for Christianity. The Bible reveals God's heart; and the more you know God's heart, the better your preparation to serve Him. You find your ability to serve God in the Scriptures.

Some love to hear sermons, while others love to read them. Some love to listen to teachers; others love to read devotional books. But a love for the Bible is imperative in the Christian life.

One great preacher testified that as a teen, "I read the Bible at camp, at home in my room, and in study hall at school. I read it sitting on a rock by the lake and sitting on my bed." His love of the Word of God has given him power in his preaching.

If you are going to be used of God, you must love the Bible for he who loves the Word of God loves God Himself. Dr. C. I. Scofield preached the funeral of D. L. Moody and noted, "God used D. L. Moody because he believed the Bible, and he believed God blessed the Bible." Moody's sermons were filled with the Bible, and God used those sermons to revive scores of people.

5. *You develop your gifts by taking the opportunities at hand.* The Bible teaches, "Whatsoever thy hand findeth to do, do it with thy might . . ." (Ecclesiastes 9:10). We are to give instant obedience to service, especially when the opportunity arises. If there is an emergency and a Sunday School teacher is needed, do the best job you can. Don't ask, "Is my gift teaching?" When someone is needed to help set up chairs at the church, don't ask, "Is this my gift?"

Obviously this principle can't be applied in every instance. If the piano player is not there, you can't play without ability. The same goes for singing a solo. But then, people won't ask you to do what they know you are unable to do.

Faithfulness in a small capacity leads to a promotion in God's sight. Jerry Falwell preaches to millions over the Old Time Gospel Television Network, yet he began as a student at Baptist Bible College, Springfield, Missouri, by teaching one fourth grade boy at High Street Baptist Church. He faced the usual discouragements, but his faithful ministry to that one boy enabled Falwell to build the class up to 53 students before the year was over.

If you want an opportunity to preach to millions, develop your ability by preaching to a handful.

6. *You find new abilities by exercising your present gifts.* A spiritual ability is a gift of God; exercising it is an act of stewardship. You are using what is God's. "As every man hath received the gift, even so minister the same one to another, as good stewards of the manifold grace of God" (I Peter 4:10).

Paul told young Timothy, "Neglect not the gift that is in thee" (I Timothy 4:14). If God entrusts you with one or several gifts, now is the time for you to obey.

When you use your gift(s), it may inspire others. Your witness for Christ will help others to have boldness in their witness. Your counsel may help someone else through a difficulty.

God expects us to grow in our ability to use our gifts and in our capacity to accept new ones. Don't be satisfied with your current abilities but grow in service.

7. *Your gifts are developed by determination.* Your determination is the key to the development of your gifts. Study to improve yourself so you can grow in the effectiveness of your gifts; you can even find new gifts you have not previously used. Enroll in courses given at church or at a local Bible college. You might study music, teaching, soul-winning, speech, or a variety of other subjects which will develop your gifts.

The difference between the few and the crowd is determination. The man that God uses is the one who is determined to be the best and do the most for Jesus Christ. And God gives the strength for success: "I can do all things through Christ which strengtheneth me" (Philippians 4:13).

Chapter 12

Winning Others To Christ

A little boy in Sunday School asked, "How can Jesus fit into my heart? He's so big." The small imagination knew that Christ was large because Christ was God.

While the teacher was trying to decide how to reply, again the small boy blurted out, "He must spill over!"

Out of the mouths of children proceeds wisdom. He was wrong on the physical size of Christ, but he was truthful on the results of salvation. The new Christian spills the love of Christ out of gratitude. This chapter analyzes the "overflow" which is the Christian's responsibility in order to reach others.

There are two emphases in evangelism; you should try to follow both. First, there is witnessing, called sharing Christ with others. Second, there is personal evangelism, called soul-winning.

Bill Adams came to know Christ when his foreman talked to him. Bill wanted to be a witness, so each Sunday morning with Bibles in hand, he and his family drove to church. At work he used his sense of humor to let the other guys know he didn't appreciate filthy jokes. He told his relatives how he found Christ. Adams wanted his testimony to be an influence on others and it was. Bill is a witness who shares with others what he has seen, heard and experienced.

When a person takes the witness stand in court he is not allowed to give his opinion or hearsay evidence. A witness only shares what he has experienced. Peter and John gave a witness before the Jewish council: "For we cannot but speak the things which we have seen and heard" (Acts 4:20). Witnessing is the first step in reaching others.

Dave Stonfield was a ministerial student with a burden for the lost on their way to hell. In chapel he asked for prayer as he went home during the holidays. He had a list of four people he wanted to win to Christ. Dave phoned, made an appointment with each person, then tried to lead them to Christ. Stonfield is a soul-winner.

A soul-winner goes beyond witnessing. He presents the gospel in a clear way so the person understands it. Then he tries to persuade that person to receive Christ.

A witness is like a factory representative who goes to the client to display his merchandise. The soul-winner is a salesman who tries to get the signature on the bottom line. Both Bill Adams and Dave Stonfield want to reach others for Christ. Both want to obey the scriptural command to evangelize.

Jesus commanded His followers to be witnesses before ascending to Heaven, as recorded in Acts 1:8—"But ye shall receive power, after that the Holy Ghost is come upon you; and ye shall be witnesses unto me both in

Jerusalem, and in all Judaea, and in Samaria, and unto the uttermost part of the earth." This verse has provided an outline for the expansion of the church of Jesus Christ.

BE A WITNESS FOR CHRIST

Witnessing may be by example or by expression, and it ought to be by both. Silent witnessing should be backed up by vocal witnessing, and what is said must be backed up by a person's life.

1. *A believer witnesses to others by the way he lives.* There ought to be a difference between sinners and saints in the way they look and act. A Christian should not be dirty, poorly-groomed, sloppily-dressed, or boorish in his actions. He should not be mastered by evil habits. He should not be willfully stupid, lazy, or irritating.

If he expresses the fruit of the Spirit, he will be loving, joyful, peaceable, patient, gentle, good, faithful, meek, and self-disciplined (Galatians 5:22-23). When he is controlled by the Holy Spirit it won't be long before others will realize there is something special about him, and that he is the kind of person they enjoy knowing. The influence of a good silent witness will cause people to conclude that the individual practices what he believes.

2. *A believer also witnesses to others by the way he talks.* Profanity, gossip, foolish jesting, telling dirty jokes, constant complaining, and other sins of the mouth drive people away from Christ. That's the negative part, however; there is a positive aspect, too. A believer is expected to talk about good things, especially the things of the Lord and His Word. New converts often find it difficult to keep quiet about their salvation experience, while those who have been saved a long time often find it difficult to say anything about their experience. Witnessing should be a lifelong habit for each Christian.

3. *A good way to begin reaching the unsaved is to give your testimony, telling what God has done for you.* Tell about your life before you were saved, how you came to Christ, and what Christ means to you now. Your testimony may be a natural entrance to present the gospel; witnessing may open the door to soul-winning.

BE A SOUL WINNER

God might have chosen angels to evangelize the world, but He did not. Angels cannot effectively be His witness because they cannot know experientially what it is to be redeemed from sin. God wanted *men* to witness to men, to be soul-winners, because we know firsthand the agony of sin and the ecstasy of salvation. We can best relate to those who are bound in sin.

1. *Soul-winning is the Christian's responsibility.* We might borrow God's words given to the prophet Ezekiel to explain our responsibility to our fellowmen: "When I say unto the wicked, Thou shalt surely die; and thou givest him not warning, nor speakest to warn the wicked from his wicked way, to save his life; the same wicked man shall die in his iniquity; but his blood will I require at thine hand" (Ezekiel 3:18).

2. *There are many forms of soul-winning.* Evangelism may be done through mass meetings, church programs, home Bible studies, county or state fair booths, gospel films, radio and television, printed literature, institutions, open-air meetings, house-to-house visitation, and many others. Most of these forms of soul-winning offer willing workers opportunities to participate.

3. *Individual soul-winning opportunities.* A point to remember is that all evangelism eventually comes down to a one-to-one encounter between a sinner seeking salvation and a soul-winner showing him the way. Every believer should know how to lead a person to Christ.

Having a plan of salvation memorized before you talk with a person makes a soul-winner more confident. One of the easiest plans to follow is found in the book of Romans, called "The Roman Road of Salvation." Mark these four verses in your Bible and commit them to memory and use them when showing someone how to be saved.

First, the fact of sin. "For all have sinned, and come short of the glory of God" (Romans 3:23). You must convince a person of his need before you can get him to accept help. A person must see that he is lost before he will seek salvation. Point out that *all* includes him; he is a sinner before God. Don't become self-righteous; include yourself. You are still a sinner, but a sinner saved by the grace of God. Don't go on to the next step until he is convinced of his need of salvation.

Second, the fact of penalty. "For the wages of sin is death; but the gift of God is eternal life through Jesus Christ our Lord" (Romans 6:23). A person will suffer the penalty because of his sin. Point out to him the opposite meaning of the words *wages* and *gift*. A person works for wages which are rightfully his. A person who serves sin will get the wages of death, which is eternal punishment. The opposite of wages is a gift, which is something that is not deserved. A gift is free. The gift of God is eternal life. A person can't work for God's gift; he must accept it, just as a child accepts a birthday present from his parents.

Third, the fact of provision. "But God commendeth his love toward us, in that, while we were yet sinners, Christ died for us" (Romans 5:8). The first step tells us we are sinners; the second step tells us that sinners die. The third step shows that Christ died as a substitute for sinners. Show the person how Christ took his place. The word *commendeth* means give, which is the verb form of the noun gift.

God gave us a gift, which was His Son who died for us. But knowing this fact is not enough, a person must accept it and believe it.

Fourth, the fact of acceptance. "That if thou shalt confess with thy mouth the Lord Jesus, and shalt believe in thine heart that God hath raised him from the dead, thou shalt be saved" (Romans 10:9). The gospel will save a person but he must believe it. He must believe that Christ not only died but was raised from the dead. When the person believes the above and accepts Jesus into his heart, he must confess publicly. He usually does this by walking forward in a church service and submitting to believers' baptism.

LEARN HOW TO REACH OTHERS

Here are some suggestions which should prove helpful in evangelism. It should be mentioned, of course, that human beings are very complicated creatures and not every technique is going to be workable in every situation.

1. *Try to rid your mind of all feelings of superiority toward sinners.* As you pray about reaching your friends, ask the Lord to make you constantly aware that you are only a sinner saved by grace. Try also to rid your mind of a feeling of sentimental pity, for this will result in a patronizing attitude. Just plan to meet people as they are, to share the Good News.

2. *Determine that you are going to be courteous and tactful in your dealings with others to whom you witness.* People sometimes are offended when they think you don't accept them as they are. They may resent the fact you talk to them about sin, sorrow for sin, repentance, and seeking forgiveness, because they think they are pretty good as they are. They might get irritated. Some won't even talk to you.

Regardless of what happens, you have to keep calm

and not lash back. If you are too aggressive, you may lose them altogether. Dallas Billington, pastor of Akron Baptist Temple, told me, "Don't pick green fruit." We can push for a decision too soon. What can't be said today might find a hearing another day. You cannot force anyone into the kingdom. The Holy Spirit must be allowed to handle the timing.

3. *It is important to get acquainted with the person first, asking him or her about personal interests.* If you immediately begin to press home the claims of Christ, you may alienate him. This establishing of rapport also gives you an opportunity to pick up useful information about the person which will be helpful when you do steer the conversation around to spiritual things.

4. *Try to find out how much the person knows about the Bible, church life, and Christian living.* You have to begin where you find him. If he is an atheist or an agnostic, you may discover he has only a fragmented and perhaps garbled understanding of such things. If he is a Jew, you might be able to meet on common ground as far as the Old Testament is concerned and go from there. If he is a Roman Catholic, you will have some beliefs in common even though you will differ on the basic issue of salvation. If he is a member of one of the false cults, you will have to have some knowledge of its teachings. The same will be true if he is a liberal Protestant.

5. *Make sure any show of interest on the part of the unsaved person is not misinterpreted.* Some individuals will be friendly and courteous to the extent that you may conclude that they are ready to make a decision for Christ, but they may not be ready to do that yet. Their eternal destiny is more important than what they think of you. If the Spirit of God impresses on you the fact that a person *is* ready to yield to Christ, then press for a decision. Review what you have said about being saved, so

you are sure he understands what is involved, then pray with him.

6. *Be sure to follow through on a new convert.* Since you led this new convert to Christ it is your responsibility to follow up on him. Just as a baby is helpless, this babe in Christ needs your love, guidance and protection. In the Great Commission, we are commanded to "make disciples . . ." (Matthew 28:19, ASV), to teach those who are saved in the ways of their new life. We are told to baptize them, thus providing an outward sign of an inward change, letting the world know they have entered into a new way of life.

Help to anchor this new convert to Christ firmly to the Scriptures, seeing that he has the witness of the Spirit, that he is a child of God. Discuss with him the fruit of the Spirit expected in the life of a believer. Show him that in obedience to Christ's command he should be baptized and taken into the church membership. Assure him of your willingness to continue to help him in his spiritual growth as a Christian.

DON'T NEGLECT SOUL-WINNING

If every Christian were faithfully winning souls as he should be, we could turn the world upside down for Christ. That is what happened in the first century. After persecution of the church in Jerusalem, it was said of the believers, "Therefore they that were scattered abroad went every where preaching the word" (Acts 8:4). Angry Jews in Thessalonica dragged believers before the magistrates of their city and said, "These that have turned the world upside down are come hither also" (Acts 17:6). Actually, the Christians were only trying to turn the world *right side up!*

Part V

Developing Inner Virtues

Chapter 13
Be Motivated by Faith, Love, Hope

Three great qualities in the Christian's life are faith, love, and hope. The Apostle Paul closed his challenging discourse on love with these words: "And now abideth faith, hope, charity [love], these three; but the greatest of these is charity [love]" (I Corinthians 13:13). You acquire faith from the Bible, love by giving, and hope from your experience.

FAITH, BASED ON THE BIBLE

Faith, we are told, is a firm belief in something or someone even when there is no proof. Some people say they cannot believe in God because they have no proof that God exists. They only need to look around them for abundant evidence that God exists, "For the invisible things of him from the creation of the world are clearly seen, being understood by the things that are made, even his eternal power and Godhead; so that they are without excuse" (Romans 1:20).

We find the basis of our faith, however, in the Bible where several aspects of faith are shown.

1. *Our salvation is by faith.* Romans 3 shows us that our redemption or salvation, though undeserved because we are sinners (verse 23), was provided for us by God through grace (verse 24), to be received by us through faith in the blood of Jesus Christ by whom we are declared righteous (verse 25).

2. *We live by faith.* If you are going to live a successful life for God, you must live it by faith. Jesus said you can move mountains if you have faith (Mark 11:23). This means you can overcome the obstacles of mountains in your life and live for God. You can apply your talents and influence lives for God. You can claim His strength and overcome the mountain of nagging habits.

Speaking of moving mountains, I believe Jerry Falwell has more faith than any other person I know. When we were beginning Lynchburg Baptist College, we speculated on the number of students we might have that first year. I hoped for 50, he said 200. I had been a college president and knew how hard it was to recruit students. I looked at the task from experience; he viewed it by faith. There were 153 day-school students that first year.

The other day I heard Falwell say his goal for the college is now 50,000 students. That means the college will be as big as the town! That's faith.

Once we were setting goals for Sunday School attendance in the church. Jerry said we could have 10,000 pupils in a small town in the Virginia foothills. By every conceivable formula of man, the goal was impossible; but with faith and hard work we had a record-breaking attendance of 10,187.

Faith centers on God, not on our ability to perceive Him. When an art student visited a museum, he spent all his time cleaning and adjusting his glasses. He also studied the layout of the museum to find the best spot from which to observe the famous paintings. He spent so much time on himself that he lost sight of the paintings. If you have tried to increase your faith and nothing has happened, perhaps you are spending too much energy on yourself. Maybe you have forgotten the focus of your faith.

Most people mistakenly think that faith is only tied to our understanding . . . that a person believes only what he can rationalize. Since faith is moral, lack of faith is an ethical problem. Many people can't put their faith in God for the same reason a thief can't find a policeman. They don't want to live by faith because of their sin. The Bible calls this "an evil heart of unbelief" (Hebrews 3:12). An atheist once told Paul Little, an evangelist to college students, "If I believed in God, I'd have to change the way I live."

Christians have difficulty believing God for the same reason. A Sunday School teacher once told me, "I wish I had the kind of faith you have." At first I was flattered, then I realized it costs to have faith. Faith is tied to repentance and consistent Bible study. The Sunday School teacher wasn't willing to pay the price to have more faith.

"Faith is the substance of things hoped for, the evidence of things not seen," said the Apostle Paul in his great faith chapter, Hebrews 11. Read in this chapter about all those heroes of faith who acted in faith in God and "obtained a good report." We Christians owe much to them and are guided in our life of faith by reading about them in the Bible.

We pray in faith, based on our confidence in God, asking whatsoever we desire according to His will. "And this is the confidence that we have in him, that, if we ask any thing according to his will, he heareth us; And if we know that he hear us, whatsoever we ask, we know that we have the petitions that we desired of him" (I John 5:14-15).

3. *We should have faith in spite of doubts.* The opposite of faith is doubt. Christians sometimes find themselves doubting God or Jesus Christ or something in the Bible. To be doubtful is to be uncertain, suspicious, or unbelieving. Considering these shades of meaning, we need to be careful about condemning everyone who admits having doubts. There is nothing wrong in being uncertain until there is time to prove truth. However, beware of a heart of unbelief when it involves what is obviously true.

If doubts should trouble you, prayerfully probe your heart to search out the origin of your doubts.

One source of doubt is ignorance. You may not know enough about God or His ways to have the faith you need. It is one thing to say that God is all-powerful, but it is something else again to really believe God will use His power to solve our problems. It is one thing to say God is loving, but it is something else again to believe He loves everyone, especially someone we may not love. It is one thing to say God answers prayer, but it is something else again to believe He is going to answer a specific request we have.

Another source of our doubts is fear. We are reluctant to express faith in certain situations because we are afraid we will be embarrassed if we don't get what we have voiced. The child jumping off a ledge into the arms of his father may hesitate for a while through fear that the father cannot or for some reason will not break his fall. When fear is gone, he jumps. Trust in our Heavenly Father certainly should be greater than trust in a fallible, earthly father.

A third source of our doubts is rebellion. It is amazing how the human mind refuses to believe what it doesn't want to believe. We have difficulty believing God because we love sin more in many cases. Maybe you doubt because you know in your heart you have disobeyed His commands, and when God sheds new light, you may question it simply because you are unwilling as yet to obey it. Sometimes we repress our sin, pushing it back into our subconscious, and hope we will not have to deal with it. We cannot sin in our heart and trust God at the same time. Eventually the sin must be faced. Yet sometimes you doubt, even when you try your hardest to believe.

Satan is adept at using all three tactics to make Christians doubt the truths of God. The devices of ignorance, fear, and rebellion are common tools in his hands. If you are suffering from a period of doubting, read II Corinthians 2:11; be aware of Satan's tactics and don't let him gain an advantage over you. There is help for you.

Ignorance is overcome by a combination of knowing the Bible and knowing how God works in our life. Read your Bible faithfully and prayerfully and seek out a dependable Bible study class or a book or course of systematic study of God's Word.

Fear is overcome by learning to trust the Lord to protect us. Look for a mature Christian, one you can talk with, who can lead you into a fuller trust in Jesus Christ in your daily life.

Rebellion is overcome by surrendering to God and His will for you. Be constantly on guard against a spirit of unbelief in your heart.

THE GREATEST VIRTUE IS LOVE

The ultimate indication that you are a Christian is your love: "We know that we have passed from death unto life, because we love the brethren" (I John 3:14). Possibly one of your most difficult tasks as a new Christian will be to learn how to love. Many older Christians, in length of time since they were saved, have been slow in learning to love. Love is the nature of God, and we must love to be like Him. Love is the basic rule of the church, and we must love others to be God-honoring Christians.

The following principles will point you toward love and increasing love in your life, but they will never produce it.

1. *Study love in the Scriptures.* In a concordance look up every reference to the word *love.* Notice that Jesus commands, "A new commandment I give unto you, That ye love one another; as I have loved you . . ." (John 13:34). Later He reaffirms this statement, "This is my commandment, That ye love one another, as I have loved you" (John 15:12). You should love other Christians for many reasons, especially because God motivates you to love others. "Ye yourselves are taught of God to love one another" (I Thessalonians 4:9).

2. *Study the nature of love.* You will probably spend the rest of your life studying the nature of love. Love is an experience. You can't put it in a test tube and analyze it. Like quicksilver, as soon as you think you have corralled it, love escapes. Maybe the problem is our definition of love. We place emphasis on the results we seek rather than on the conditions that bring about those results. We think that love is feelings. But love is deeper than that—it expresses feelings in action. When God chose to love you, He went beyond the deep feelings of His heart; He died for you. When you love your kids, you go beyond the feelings of your heart. You work, teach, and sacrifice for them.

Jesus said, "Love your enemies." Loving your enemies is more than the right feeling in your heart. You must do the right thing toward them. Jesus taught us how to love our enemies. On the cross He uttered, "Father forgive them . . ." Jesus looked into the faces of those who had spit on Him and crowned Him with thorns. He saw those who had slapped Him in the face, scourged Him, and made Him carry the cross to Golgotha. Still He said, "Forgive them." That's love.

Love is not getting; it's giving. Love is giving your life to the one you love. Jesus said, "Greater love hath no man than this, that a man lay down his life for his friends" (John 15:13). When you give of yourself, you are loving the other person. John told us how to understand love. "Hereby perceive we the love of God, because he laid down his life for us: and we ought to lay down our lives for the brethren" (I John 3:16).

When a young man and woman get married, they pledge their love to each other. They give themselves to each other. This is hard to do, but this is love.

Today's young people think that love is easy because they think love is getting. They are wrong. Lust is getting, but love is giving. You can give without loving, but you can't love without giving. If you love God, you will change yourself for Him (Romans 12:1-2).

3. *Understand love's demands.* Love is a relationship of giving in which you give up your rights and your selfish pleasures. You accept others, even the ones you don't like.

"But I'm only human," you complain, "it's hard to love my boss." Don't make excuses for your bitterness and hatred. It is hard to love some people; you may have to work at it. With other people, love comes easy. But it is never right for a Christian to be bitter.

Christians ought to be different from and purer than

the world. Because you live by Christ's standards, you should be different. Because you have Christ in your heart, you should be purer. As a Christian, you should be characterized by love.

As a group, no people are more alike than Christians. Is it their love that draws them together? When a born-again believer walks into a crowd, he can usually spot another Christian. As ministers travel from church to church, they meet new people and make friends. A traveling Bible teacher once remarked that as soon as he got into the car of a fellow believer, they became friends. He noted, "We struck up an immediate friendship as though we had known each other all our lives, yet there are unsaved people in my city that I know, with whom I have little in common." A deep love for Jesus Christ makes the difference. Because He is in both hearts, Christ gives a mutual love one to the other.

The early Christians manifested love. Josephus, who lived among the early Christians, said, "Oh, how they love each other." Sometimes it is easier to see a Christian's love over nineteen centuries than it is to look across the street. That's because we see better at a far distance.

There are times, however, when the Christian should hate. You should never hate people, but the sins of people. Sometimes it is difficult to hate the sin without hating the sinner, but it must be done. Love and Scripture teach you how to draw the line.

4. *Beware of false dreams of love.* A "false dream" expects love to be like strawberry shortcake. Mature love does not expect an easy life. The early disciples expected a hard life but when they followed Jesus they had no idea how high the cost would be. He had told them to leave father, mother; as a matter of fact, He said to leave all. Their love led them to endure many trials.

A God of love does not allow us to sidestep hardships. He is more concerned with our character than our comfort. The Bible teaches that persecution brings about character. Tribulation increases patience. God still uses the spade of sorrow to dig the well of joy. Perhaps we don't have many men of Job's character because we don't have many men afflicted as Job.

A mother misunderstood God's love when her son died of cancer. She complained that God was mean. "Where was God when my son died?" she cried.

"Right where He was when His son died," the wise pastor answered. "Sitting on His throne."

God loves everyone. We don't understand why He took the young boy with cancer. We can't explain why God left the woman lonely. But God sits on His throne and knows that " . . . all things work together for good to them that love God . . ." (Romans 8:28).

HOPE, THE MOTIVATING VIRTUE

Everyone wants better conditions—a better job . . . a better car . . . a better house. We live with the *hope* that things will get better. Hope is the most powerful of all virtues because it motivates us to continued faith.

God puts hope in your heart when you are saved. You exercise this hope by exercising faith. "Faith is the substance of things hoped for . . ." (Hebrews 11:1). Hope is the medicine that cures depression and gives us patience to endure trials.

1. *You can have hope because of Christ's presence in your life.* Jesus challenged His disciples to "Abide in me, and I in you" (John 15:4). The presence of Christ in your heart can help you to overcome anything. That makes life worth living. But more than His power in your heart, you must place yourself in Him. Jesus emphasized that we should abide in Him. This involves reading His Word,

fellowshipping with Him in prayer and obeying His commandments.

Constant fellowship with Jesus Christ is the normal Christian life. Perhaps we have lived in a subnormal state so long that mediocrity is considered normal. This isn't the way it should be.

A man walking out of a smoke-filled nightclub asked, "What's that I smell?" His friend replied, "Fresh air." He had become accustomed to the pollution. In the same way, many Christians are shocked to find that Christ can give them victory over the pollution of sin.

God wants His children to be successful. He told Joshua, "Be strong and of a good courage: for unto this people shalt thou divide for an inheritance the land . . ." (Joshua 1:6). The Lord tied spiritual hope to subduing their enemies.

"This book of the law shall not depart out of thy mouth; but thou shalt meditate therein day and night, that thou mayest observe to do according to all that is written therein: For then thou shalt make thy way prosperous, and then thou shalt have good success" (Joshua 1:8). God has no enjoyment when you fail or quit. He rejoices with every success. Hope is enjoying the victory you will receive. Worry is self-defeating; it usually guarantees exactly the thing you worry about.

2. *You should have hope because all things work together for good.* Discouragement is nothing more than the collapse of a Christian's hope. "Things can't improve," a woman says. She fears the future just like the man who maintains, "Things are gonna get worse."

A middle-aged man drags a steel brace around on his leg because he had polio as a boy. He could have been bitter because he never played sports. But he has accepted everything as being from God. Each week he anticipates God's work in his life. He knows that one day he will walk without crutches and a brace, and his struggle with pain will be over. Hope conquers all.

The Bible teaches, "And we know that all things work together for good to them that love God . . ." (Romans 8:28). God has His hand on the controls. You might not like everything that happens to you, but God is never caught by surprise.

When you know the Scriptures, you will live daily with the anticipation of God's working in your life. "For whatsoever things were written aforetime were written for our learning, that we through patience and comfort of the scriptures might have hope" (Romans 15:4). The total message of Scripture produces optimistic living. You have a bright future with each day's dawning. Even when circumstances do not get better, God's grace is sufficient for every need. When your life is in His hands, there are no emergencies with which He cannot cope.

Perhaps you are going through tribulation now. It is necessary for everyone to go through the waters of sacrifice at some time . . . it mellows us and makes us depend on Him. Through the tribulation, we learn to hope in God. "But if we hope for that we see not, then do we with patience wait for it" (Romans 8:25).

3. *You should have hope because you will go to Heaven when you die.* Jesus promised that He was preparing a place for us in Heaven (that's hope) and that He would come back to get us when we die (that's hope abundant). "Let not your heart be troubled . . . I go to prepare a place for you. And if I go and prepare a place for you, I will come again, and receive you unto myself; that where I am, there ye may be also" (John 14:1-3). The martyr testified, "I'd rather live short and die right than live long and die wrong."

The Christain is not primarily concerned with, "How long can I live?" His concern is, "How good can I live?"

Hope makes the difference. The more hope you have, the more indifferent you become to problems here below.

4. *You should have hope because Christ is coming for you.* A little girl went to her mother with a ribbon. "Fix my hair," she asked.

"You don't usually like me to fix your hair," the mother said, perplexed because she had tried to teach her daughter to look pretty for others, but she had resisted.

"My Sunday School teacher said Jesus can come at any time, and I want to be ready for Him," the little girl answered.

The Bible teaches that we should live, "looking for that blessed hope, and the glorious appearing of the great God and our Saviour Jesus Christ" (Titus 2:13). Hope that Christ is coming for you will help you get through any problem.

Hope is manufactured out of a realization that God sits on the throne. What a comfort it is to the Christian to know that He is in control.

Chapter 14

Be Faithful All Your Days

One of the greatest abilities in life is "stickability." The Bible teaches that stickability is faithfulness. It is "required in stewards, that a man be found faithful" (I Corinthians 4:2). Faithfulness is obeying Jesus Christ.

A conductor, beginning his new appointment to an orchestra said, "I'd rather have ten members of an orchestra that were faithful than have a 100-piece orchestra that I couldn't depend on.

Following this same theme, a minister announced he would rather have a church of 200 people who were faithful in soul-winning and prayer than a church with 1,800 members in which only a handful showed up for prayer meeting.

Faithful Christians will receive rewards. Jesus said,

"Behold I come quickly; and my reward is with me, to give every man according as his work shall be" (Revelation 22:12). Martyrs faithful unto death will receive the crown of life (Revelation 2:10). When the sword was pointed in their direction, they did not deny Jesus Christ. Perhaps they were told to stop witnessing in the name of Jesus Christ, but they continued. The Scripture doesn't tell us how many souls they won, but it does tell us they were faithful to death.

Many Christians think they cannot serve God. They look at their talents and feel they have too little ability to serve Him. A minister once said, "You may not be much . . . but you can be faithful. The greatest need in the church today is people who are faithful—faithful in living, service, prayer, and tithing."

God uses the thermometer of faithfulness to test the temperature of our love. You don't store up faithfulness like saving money to spend on a vacation. Faithfulness is not what you get as a result of being good. Faithfulness is what you are. We cannot prepare to be faithful, nor can we educate ourselves into faithfulness. The farmers used to say, "He who waits to be faithful will never get started."

Becoming faithful starts with new motivation; it can't be worked up. Christ makes you faithful. When He lives His life through you, you are in the process of becoming faithful.

BECOMING FAITHFUL

Faithfulness is the by-product of duty. A Christian does not seek faithfulness. He makes Christ the center of his life and his actions produce faithfulness. This same principle can be applied to the businessman who said, "I didn't set out to make money. I determined to build a good business and just happened to make money." The following points will carry you on the road of duty, hence making you faithful.

1. *Faithfulness begins to grow when you follow the clear command of Scripture.* Some things ought to be first because God said so. "But seek ye first the kingdom of God, and his righteousness" (Matthew 6:33). If you want to be happy, you must seek or pursue the things of the kingdom of God. This is seeking God's righteousness for your life. When you come to the place where you can say, *I want God in my life more than anything else in the world,* you have made the right decision.

2. *Faithfulness grows when you have an honest appraisal of yourself.* An enthusiastic ministerial candidate once said, "I'm a streamlined train going 75 miles per hour." A wise grandmother heard the boast and thought otherwise. "Be careful. Your boiler may blow up," she warned the young man after the meeting. "I've been living the Christian life for over 40 years and it's tough."

Within the human heart are two natures. The old nature seeks after selfish desires. The new nature seeks after the things of God. Recognize that these natures wrestle in your heart. You are the referee. Make sure you call a clean bout. If you are going to grow in faithfulness, your new nature will have to win daily.

Jesus said, "Ye cannot serve God and mammon" (Luke 16:13). He recognized that people would wrestle with their priorities, whether it be money or Him. You can only have one master.

When you are wise, you know how to put priorities on the correct things. "I enjoy getting my shoes shined," a businessman once said. "It's not the most important thing in life. It's a small thing. But I like to look neat." He had placed things in their proper perspective.

You don't put diamonds on your shoes; you put them on your fingers. Neither do we place diamonds among rhinestones. Everything has its setting. Golf, dating, and driving a new car each has its place; but driving a new car to the sacrifice of an education is a mistake. You must know yourself; and faithfulness begins when you be yourself.

3. *Faithfulness is personified in your determination.* Faithfulness is doing your duty because it should be done. Antipas is buried in the Christian's tomb of the unknown soldier because he was faithful. Nothing else is known about him. We don't know if Antipas was a preacher, evangelist, or church janitor. We don't know if he was a new Christian or had lived a long, faithful life. All we know is that the Scriptures say, "Antipas was my faithful martyr" (Revelation 2:13). Because Antipas was faithful, he was killed. A minister once said, "Out of all the martyrs God knows (and God knows them all), He wanted to include Antipas because he was killed for his faithfulness."

Faithfulness is doing what needs to be done. If an announcement was made from the pulpit that the church lawn needed mowing, the faithful man would do it.

Recently a pastor phoned one of his deacons at 1:00 A.M. and requested he make a hospital call with him. When asked why he called him, the pastor said, "Because I knew I could count on you." He was faithful.

Jesus was faithful. The Bible says He ". . . went about doing good . . ." (Acts 10:38). Jesus was in perfect control of all circumstances because He was in perfect control of Himself.

Every choice you make molds your future. Past choices have already affected you, and present choices will affect you and those around you.

Faithfulness is the mental attitude that you will never give up. The French Foreign Legion is supposed to have said:

"If I falter in battle, push me forward.
"If I stumble in battle, pick me up.
"If I faint in battle, revive me.
"If I retreat from battle, shoot me."

A country boy was hired to work on the railroad. He was told, "Take this steel pole, go by and hit each wheel on every train that comes into this station." He was looking for trouble spots. For 37 years, he took his pole and hit every wheel of every train that came into the yard. When he retired they asked if he knew why he was hitting the tires.

"No, sir," he responded. When asked why he had done what he did not understand for 37 years, he replied, "I just did what they told me." While we might not admire his intelligence, we can applaud his faithfulness.

You might question why God allows some of His people to go through hard times. Sometimes God is testing their faith to make it grow. Other times it seems He is trying to find out if any is there!

4. *Faithfulness must add wisdom to determination.* Bullheaded determination will not make you faithful. The man who butts his head against the wall usually gets bloody. You are faithful when you do the proper thing for the proper reason. If you have failed many times, this does not mean you cannot become faithful. Everyone has failed in some things. Don't let your defeat discourage you. No one learns as much from his successes as from his failures. Edison was once asked, "Why didn't you quit after 780 failures?"

"I've not failed 780 times but learned that 780 things don't work in a light bulb." You can't stop a spirit that won't quit.

A great preacher met an agnostic on a narrow footbridge. The agnostic glowered at Wesley, "I never step aside for a fool."

"I always do," answered Wesley. He was faithful to God, yet wise enough not to get involved in a needless fight.

STEADFAST FAITHFULNESS

Solomon says, "A faithful man who can find?" (Proverbs 20:6). In a day when men change with the blowing wind, it is hard to find a man who is faithful to God. But those who are faithful to God have His blessing. "A faithful man shall abound with blessings" (Proverbs 28:20). To get the anointing of God upon our lives, we don't have to be flashy or sensational, just remain steadfastly faithful.

There was a wedding in Cana of Galilee. No one remembers the bride, what she wore, or who attended the ceremony. Yet Christ's presence made it the best known ceremony in all eternity. Just as Christ's presence immortalized the wedding in Cana, so His indwelling will make you faithful. People will forget what Sunday School class you taught and the size of your paycheck, but your faithfulness will live on forever.

There were many dusty bushes in the Sinai desert. Today no one cares about them. But we remember the flaming bush from which God spoke to Moses. God's presence immortalized one dry bush so that every child in Sunday School knows about it. When God indwells our lives, we stand apart from humanity.

Faithfulness is not only worshiping Christ. It involves the active life. Moses communed with God in the burning bush, but that was not enough. If he had simply enjoyed the presence of God, God's people would have perished in bondage. Faithfulness was putting his shoes on and going to Egypt.